A Shelter Is Not a Home...
Or Is It?

REVISITED

White Tiger Press—New York

Also from the Institute for Children, Poverty, and Homelessness:

The New Poverty: Homeless Families in America
Hopes, Dreams & Promise: The Future of Homeless Children in America
Moving Out, Moving Up: Families Beyond Shelter
Beyond the Shelter Wall: Homeless Families Speak Out
The American Family Inn Handbook—A How To Guide

A Shelter Is Not a Home...
Or Is It?

REVISITED

Ralph da Costa Nunez
President of the Institute for Children, Poverty, and Homelessness

Foreword by

Leonard N. Stern
Founder of Homes for the Homeless

Library of Congress Cataloging-in-Publication Data

Book design: Alice Fisk MacKenzie
Cover design: James Farnam

ISBN 9780-9825533-0-5

©2010
Institute for Children, Poverty, and Homelessness
This edition published 2012
White Tiger Press
50 Cooper Square, 4th Floor
New York, NY 10003

A White Tiger Book

Printed in the United States of America

The definition of insanity is doing the same thing
over and over again
and expecting different results.

—Albert Einstein

Table of Contents

Figures and Tables

Foreword

As I look today at the issue of family homelessness, I realize that the more some things change, in the end, the more they stay the same. The story of homelessness, for me, is a journey that began over two decades ago when Edward Koch, who was then the mayor of New York City, and I visited the Roberto Clemente family shelter in the Bronx. Until that time I had no idea what homelessness really was. Like most New Yorkers, I thought the homeless were grown men, and in some cases women, who had mental illnesses, or substance abuse problems, or were simply down on their luck. You would see them on the street corners, on park benches, or sleeping in doorways, and you would almost always try to avoid them.

On that evening in the autumn of 1985, when I walked into the Clemente shelter, I was stunned. I could not believe that entire families with children were also homeless. I would soon learn that they are the fastest growing segment of the homeless population; the Clemente shelter made that obvious. The facility was a large gymnasium converted into a makeshift shelter. There were hundreds of cots pushed together on an open floor, with congregate bathrooms and fluorescent lights that stayed on all night. Everywhere you looked there were state troopers standing guard, and there was nothing about the place that would make anyone feel safe or glad to be there.

It was then that I decided that something more must be done, and that the public at large needed to know that homelessness was also about children. With the help of Mayor Koch and his administration, along with the Rev. James Parks Morton of the Cathedral of St. John the Divine, I established Homes for the Homeless: a not-for-profit organization that would immediately begin providing clean, safe, and humane transitional housing for homeless families with children until they secured a permanent housing placement.

In 1986 we opened our first facility, the Prospect Family Inn, formerly a private proprietary hospital in the Bronx. Over the next few months we would open two more Inns—the Saratoga Family Inn in Queens and the Island Family Inn in Staten Island. In less than a year we housed twice the number of families that I saw at the Clemente shelter and 12% of the city's overall family shelter population. As time went on, I began to understand that homelessness is about something more than just housing. It is a symptom of a severe, debilitating poverty. The families who came to our Inns were not just there because they needed a place to live; they had all kinds of social needs.

Over the last seventeen years I have met women who were the victims of domestic violence; people who wanted to go to work, but just didn't have the skills; and very young mothers, with young children caught up in a calamity of events—not understanding how they got there and not knowing where they were going next. Above all else, however, it is children that moved me to do something about the scourge of homelessness. Although homelessness affects people of all ages, it is the children who are the real victims and their numbers continue to grow. Today, there are more children in New York City shelters than there are adults, and the typical homeless person in the city is now a young child.

In a nation that prides itself on the well-being of its children, we as a society need to ensure that homeless children have a future and a chance to learn, play, and experience childhood. Nothing is more disheartening than hearing a child say, "When I grow up, I'm going to be a teacher, a fireman, a nurse, or a lawyer," and to know that their hopes and dreams may never come true without support. That support has been the mission of Homes for the Homeless.

When my journey into the work of homelessness began, I never imagined that it would continue for so long. Four mayors have come and gone, each grappling with this issue in his own way. Some built more shelters; others closed them. Despite new initiatives and efforts, homelessness continues to grow. In the twenty-three years since Homes for the Homeless first opened its doors, we have served over *30,000 families with 50,000 children* in our facilities. Not everyone needed all of the services we provided, but everyone benefited from something. For example, one young girl went from living at the Saratoga Family Inn to college and beyond. Only she and her mother lived together in shelter; her three siblings were all in alternative care. Her mother went through our job-training program and eventually got a job. The girl excelled in our accelerated after-school programs, and was accepted into the Bronx School of Science, one of New York's most competitive and elite high schools. The young girl and her mother moved into permanent housing, and brought the whole family back together. The young girl — now a young woman — went on to attend Bryn Mawr College, one of the nation's top women's colleges. Empowered by her own experience, one summer she even returned to work with other homeless children at the sleep-away camps Homes for the Homeless sponsors. Nonetheless, here we are; it has been five years since the first edition of this book, and family homelessness is worse than ever. In fact, New York City's family homeless policies are no longer progressive and in many ways are becoming regressive.

We have come a long way with this issue, but, obviously, we still have a long way to go. Until every homeless boy, girl, and parent stands on equal ground with equal opportunities to participate in the American Dream, our work is not done. In addition to telling the story of family homelessness in New York City, this book also provides a blueprint for the future — a new way to look at homelessness, and a way to truly begin to bring about its end. The time to understand this is now. It has been and still is my hope that one day no child or family will be homeless in America, and shelters will be a thing of the past.

Leonard N. Stern
New York City, December 2009

Preface

A Shelter Is Not a Home...Or Is It? REVISITED is the product of over twenty-four years of working with homeless families. During that period, there have been numerous plans to reduce homelessness and theories to explain its causes—first and foremost the lack of affordable housing. Yet family homelessness stubbornly persists, and it is worse today than at any time before. Each evening across America hundreds of thousands of men, women, and children sleep in abandoned buildings, tents, cars, shelters, or on the streets because they are homeless. Hundreds of thousands more live doubled and tripled up in tenuous housing situations and sometime in the future they will be homeless as well.

When will it ever end? The realities that many of these families face: histories of foster care and domestic violence, a lack of employment options and affordable housing, and multiple episodes of homelessness create a bleak picture. For the children of these families—who must transfer schools multiple times, get left back and placed into special education, and then frequently drop out of school altogether as adolescents—it is worse. *A Shelter Is Not a Home...Or Is It? REVISITED* is their ongoing story; it traces the evolution of family homelessness in New York City, the homeless capital of America. The book also measures over a quarter-century of government responses to this crisis, looks at its root causes, and offers a comprehensive, logical approach, based on these factors, to reducing family homelessness.

Today, more than ever before, family homelessness exists as a permanent part of the poverty landscape, and past experiences continue to demonstrate that housing alone will not solve the problem. If we are ever going to truly end family homelessness, we must understand that it encompasses a multitude of social ills. We also have to acknowledge that little low-income housing has been built and even less appears on the horizon. Finally, we must begin to deal with family homelessness where we have the greatest ability to have the broadest impact: in shelters where these families continue to reside. This book is a first step in the process, and New York City is still the case study that holds the answer to reducing family homelessness once and for all.

Ralph da Costa Nunez
New York City, December 2009

Acknowledgments

A Shelter Is Not a Home... Or Is It? REVISITED is the product of many years of ongoing observation, discussion, and research on family homelessness. The input of former city officials and the hard work of the staff at the Institute for Children, Poverty, and Homelessness (formerly the Institute for Children and Poverty) made the work a reality. In particular, I would like to thank Nancy Wackstein, Ken Murphy, and Larry Schatt for providing us with much government insight. I thank Sal Tuchelli, former operator of the Martinique Hotel, for sharing his experience working with homeless families. At the Institute for Children, Poverty, and Homelessness, Elizabeth Clarke, Jesse Ellison, Erin Thompson, and Amanda Glatzel spent hours upon hours researching and organizing many aspects of this work. I am grateful to the many individuals who read and commented on the manuscript, in particular Laura Caruso and Karina Kwok. Finally, I thank Andrea Pizano, Meg Devlin O'Sullivan, and Rebecca Tublitz for their research and editing assistance in updating the second edition of the book. In the end, *A Shelter Is Not a Home... Or Is It?* REVISITED is the product of a unique and extremely supportive board of directors at both Homes for the Homeless and the Institute for Children, Poverty, and Homelessness; these individuals have always challenged us to explore the root causes of family homelessness, seek common-sense solutions, and continue to make our observations public.

Introduction

New York City serves as a beacon for those in search of prosperity, and the histories of those who helped shape the metropolis into one of the world's premier cultural and financial capitals are well known. Less well known are the stories of the many that found poverty instead of wealth. Rich and poor have long coexisted in New York; yet today, there exists a new kind of poverty—an epidemic of destitution largely hidden from public view. Family homelessness has grown exponentially in the last three decades, and its victims are the city's most vulnerable citizens: young single women and their children.

Children now make up nearly half (43%) of the total shelter population in New York City and, for the duration of their childhoods, a shelter may be their only home.[1] How did this happen? Homelessness remains one of the most misunderstood issues of our time. It is not simply a story of housing needs, but rather part of a larger picture in which social ills and economic instability created a new poverty in America.

This book tells the story of family homelessness in New York City, how it first emerged in the 1980s and came to define the urban landscape. This monograph answers the questions: Who are today's homeless families? Where do they come from? What challenges do they face? What does their future hold? How has the government responded to homelessness and why have these responses often exacerbated the problem?

When I f irst began to work with homelessness in the early eighties, in the office of then Mayor Koch, neither I, nor anyone else involved, ever thought that this crisis would continue for the next twenty years. Nor did we think it would get worse. Unfortunately, the problem has grown and demands new thinking, insights, and solutions. By examining

family homelessness in its entirety—as an all-encompassing poverty—
we have a chance to develop new policies that both make sense and make
a difference. Understanding homelessness as a chronic—and perhaps
permanent problem—in America helps us address its root causes and,
with hope, prevent more children from becoming trapped in a cycle that
has already claimed so many.

Homelessness in New York City: An Overview

Homelessness is not a new problem for New York City. At the turn of the
20th century, city leaders grappled with a 50% poverty rate. Urbanization
and immigration led to an acute overcrowding in city housing. In the
city's poorest neighborhoods, such as the Bowery, the destitute found a
night's rest on a hammock in a flophouse or inside a five-by-seven-foot
sleeping "cage" at a "cage hotel." These impoverished New Yorkers were
not just adults; beginning as early as the mid-1800s, there were an estimated 30,000 homeless children on New York's streets.[2]

Jacob Riis's seminal 1890 work, "How the Other Half Lives: Studies Among the Tenements of New York," exposed squalid tenement housing and the plight of thousands of street urchins, newsboys, and orphans.
The public outcry in response helped charitable agencies build support for
improving conditions for poor children. The Children's Aid Society orga-
nized the orphan trains, an ambitious effort that relocated over 120,000
orphaned or homeless New York City children to adoptive families in the
Western United States between 1853 and 1929.[3] In 1886, a forerunner to
today's multi-service shelter appeared when the country's first settlement
house opened on the city's Lower East Side and offered community and
social services to impoverished families.[4]

During this time, the public placed the homeless into two categories: the "worthy poor," widows, children, and elderly who were offered
relief at almshouses; and the "unworthy poor," wanderers and vagrants
assigned to workhouses. Philanthropic organizations employed what they
considered "scientific" methods to determine true need, and reformed a
system they felt gave indiscriminate charity to "tramp menaces." For example, the city's wayfarer's lodges initiated a work requirement wherein

shelter-seeking men chopped a cord of wood and shelter-seeking women scrubbed floors in exchange for a night's lodging.[5]

The distinction between the "deserving" and the "undeserving" poor soon became meaningless with the massive economic downturn of the Great Depression. During the 1930s, thousands of New Yorkers lost their jobs and many became homeless residents of shantytowns in city parks and vacant lots. The public no longer considered it a moral failing to wait in a soup kitchen line. Even the language surrounding homelessness changed as the more neutral term "transient" replaced the word "tramp."[6]

Such widespread poverty prompted President Franklin Delano Roosevelt to take action. Between 1933 and 1935 FDR unveiled the series of federal initiatives known as the New Deal. Among these programs were such make-work projects as the Civilian Conservation Corps (CCC), the Work Project Administration (WPA), and the Federal Transient Program (FTP). The latter created over 600 work camps and facilities across the nation for homeless Americans who wandered from place to place in search of employment. One of the most significant New Deal achievements was the Social Security Act of 1936 and, specifically, its Aid for Families with Dependent Children (AFDC) provision. AFDC gave states welfare grants earmarked for the poor — single mothers and children — that were then matched with state and local funds and allocated to these families for their housing, food, and clothing costs. The passage of this act yielded the country's first national welfare system.

A generation later, homelessness persisted but less visibly. In 1962, Michael Harrington's influential book, *The Other America: Poverty in the United States*, helped bring poverty back on to the national agenda and heavily influenced President Lyndon Baines Johnson's domestic policy and War on Poverty. Johnson's push to create or expand such programs as Medicaid, food stamps, Head Start, and AFDC contributed to a decline in the national poverty rate, from 22% in 1960 to approximately 14% by 1969.[7] Ultimately, however, Johnson's vision for a "great society" gave way to funding the war in Vietnam.

The 1960s also witnessed a push for the deinstitutionalization of psychiatric patients, eventually leading to the discharge of thousands of mentally ill individuals from public hospitals. Deinstitutionalization appealed to liberals, who called for the individual freedom of patients, and conservatives, who sought to cut costs by shutting down hospitals. The community-based housing and social services to facilitate these closings, however, never came to fruition. In New York, thousands of former patients ended up on city streets. Ironically, some of those former hospitals would eventually become homeless shelters, and the same clients who once had been hospital patients receiving treatment now lived in these facilities with few, if any, appropriate services.[8]

During this time, most of the homeless population was considered "chronically homeless" and "pathologically poor."[9] The typical homeless person in the city before 1980 was usually an unemployed single male adult, often with substance abuse and mental health problems. Temporarily displaced families with children made up a far smaller group of the homeless population, but in recent years, their numbers have grown. The typical homeless person in New York City today is a young child.

A New Poverty: The New Homeless

But what happened in the 1980s? How did the shift from the "old homeless"—a mentally ill, substance-abusing male—to the "new homeless"—young families and children—come about? How did emergency shelters fill beyond capacity and large old hotels become the much-criticized, crime-ridden "welfare hotels"? Why, after four mayors and numerous commissioners, could the city not get ahead of this crisis? And why, despite the millions of dollars poured into it, did the most extensive shelter system in the country remain known for its inefficiency and inadequacy, even by those city officials who created it? After more than twenty years, one has to wonder if a shelter has indeed become a home. The story that follows explores these questions by examining the evolution of family homelessness in New York City and public policy responses through the 1980s, 1990s, and into the new millennium. Only by understanding the issue within this context can we begin a dialogue on ending family homelessness. This book presents a vision for real change.

Notes

[1] New York City Department of Homeless Services, "Average Daily Shelter Census," http://www.nyc.gov/html/dhs/html/home/home.shtml

[2] Children's Aid Society, "History," http://www.childrensaidsociety.org/about/history

[3] Ibid.

[4] United Neighborhood Houses, "Settlement House History," http://unhny.org/about/settlement.cfm

[5] Kenneth L. Kusmer, *Down and Out and On the Road: The Homeless in American History* (New York: Oxford University Press, 2002), 74.

[6] Ibid., 209.

[7] U.S. Census Bureau, "Poverty 2002," http://www.census.gov/pop-profile/poverty.html

[8] E. Fuller Torrey, "Stop the Madness," *Wall Street Journal*, 18 July 1997.

[9] Senator Daniel Patrick Moynihan's much-discussed report from 1965, *The Negro Family: The Case for National Action*, helped popularize the notion of a "pathology" of poverty.

1 | The Early 1980s

A First Response to a Growing Crisis

In many ways, the 1980s was a decade of contradictions. After years of blight and decay, New York City finally started to flourish again. New immigrant groups and former suburbanites established roots in the thriving urban metropolis, while working-class businesses established themselves in the city's skyscrapers. Wall Street boasted record gains, and the real estate market saw an unprecedented building boom. New York moguls like Harry Helmsley and Donald Trump achieved fame, and the term "yuppie" (young urban professional) became a household word.

Yet this was also the decade in which the number of New Yorkers living in extreme poverty grew by alarming proportions. A crack epidemic ravaged the city's poorest neighborhoods, particularly Harlem, the South Bronx, Bushwick, and East New York. Crime was on the rise, as was the number of welfare recipients. By 1984, 927,000 people received public assistance. In 1989, the city itself was in the red and faced a $1.8 billion budget deficit.[1]

The 1980s also marked the beginning of the modern homeless crisis, with the number of homeless parents and children seeking shelter growing by leaps and bounds. In 1982, 950 families were in the city's emergency shelter system; by 1988 that figure had grown to more than 5,000, an increase of 500% (see Figure 1).[2] New York City was completely unprepared for this steady stream of homeless families. They presented an entirely new challenge to the city's conscience, budget, and capacity to serve its citizens. Historically, a small portion of the city's homeless consisted of families who had been displaced as a result of some unforeseen event such as fire or illness. The public generally perceived this subpopulation as "good" people who were temporarily down on their luck. In the 1980s, however, perceptions of homeless families shifted and espoused increasingly negative connotations—such as the myth of the welfare queen. By the end of the 1980s, with thousands of families relying on shelters, the city scrambled for a solution. At the same time, a debate arose over the possible causes for such an exponential increase: was it a lagging economy, cuts in social services, or a lack of affordable housing?

Figure 1
Average Daily Family Shelter Census (New York City, 1982 to 1988)
Source: *Mayor's Management Report, 1982 to 1988*

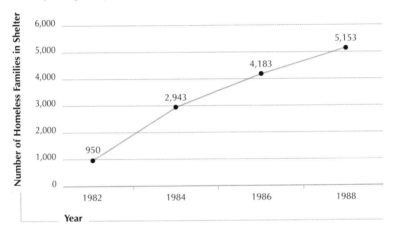

The Economy

The national economic recession in the early eighties left its mark on New York City and increased the number of families living in poverty. As the national unemployment rate reached 8%, the city's unemployment rate climbed to 10.5%, a ten-year high.[3] Especially hard hit was the manufacturing sector, an industry that had traditionally provided a viable employment avenue for New Yorkers with little or no schooling. Meanwhile, the minimum wage remained constant at $3.35 between 1981 and 1990, despite a 48% rise in the cost of living.[4]

As real incomes fell, the number of families living in poverty rose. In 1983, 27% of New York City renters lived below the poverty line, up from just over 22% in 1977. In the Bronx, 36% of renters lived below the poverty line (see Figure 2).[5] Over the same period, the poverty rate for the city's children jumped from 21% to 30%.[6] By the mid-1980s, when the economy finally began to recover and flourish, the wealthier classes, rather than low-income families, reaped the gains of the so-called Reagan economy.

Figure 2
Renter Households with Incomes Below the Poverty Level by New York City Borough (1983)
Source: *Housing and Vacancy Report: New York City,* 1983

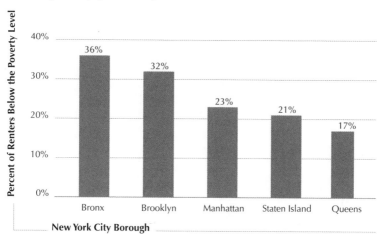

Social Service Cuts

At the same time that many New Yorkers faced unemployment and poverty, a series of public policy shifts began to undermine social service benefits. During the economic recession of the early eighties, the Reagan administration restructured the scope and delivery of social services and truncated the federal government's role in providing them. The President simultaneously increased military spending and dramatically reduced funding for social programs (see Figure 3).

Beginning with the Omnibus Budget Reconciliation Act of 1981, the administration drastically cut the budget for many traditional entitlement programs and delegated much of its social welfare responsibilities to the states. As a result, benefits for poor families, such as Aid to Families with Dependent Children (AFDC), food stamps, and housing assistance, sharply declined. Between 1970 and 1981, an average of 72% of all poor American children received AFDC; by the end of 1987, only 54% got such assistance.[7]

Other critical services also evaporated, as programs addressing drug abuse, teen pregnancy, and domestic violence were eliminated. Without federal support, low-income individuals slipped further into poverty and their drug-ravaged neighborhoods continued to deteriorate. Although the city and state did what they could to make up the difference, they had their own budget deficits with which to contend.

Figure 3
The Percent Change in Federal Spending: Social vs. Military Programs (1980 to 1990)
Source: Jobs with Peace Campaign, Fact Sheet, 1990 in Padraig O'Malley, *Homelessness: New England and Beyond,* 1992

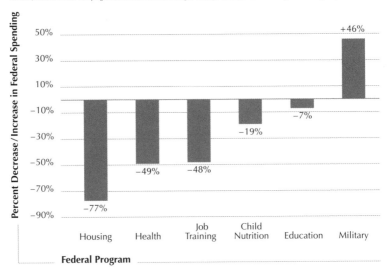

Lack of Affordable Housing

In addition to scaling back entitlement programs and benefits, the federal government also withdrew from its low-income housing efforts. The Reagan administration's budget for the Department of Housing and

Urban Development (HUD) fell from over $30 billion in 1981 to under $8 billion in 1989 (see Figure 4).[8] In New York City, those numbers translated into a $1.5 billion drop in aid.[9]

Figure 4
Decrease in HUD Budget Spending for Housing Assistance (1981 to 1989)
Source: National Low Income Housing Information Service, 1990

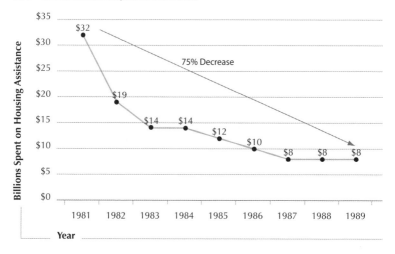

Moreover, the extremely competitive rental market in New York further exacerbated the decline in low-income housing resources. On block after city block, private interests demolished tenements and dilapidated buildings to make way for more upscale units. Between 1984 and 1987, there was a 191% increase in units renting for $1,000 or more (see Table 1).[10] Many of the buildings slated for demolition or renovation were single room occupancy units, or SROs. For very poor individuals, these humble one-room lodgings with communal bathrooms were the traditional last stopgap before homelessness.

Even middle-class New Yorkers struggled to find affordable housing. The U.S. Department of Housing and Urban Development defines the standard measure of an affordable rent as no more than 30% of a person's monthly income. When looking for an apartment, many

Table 1
Available Vacant Units by Monthly Contract Rent: New York City (1984 and 1987)
Source: *Housing and Vacancy Report: New York City,* 1987

Contract Rent	Available Units		Percent Change
Low Income Units	1984	1987	
< $300	12,856	5,836	−55%
$300 to $399	6,535	10,115	+55%
Total	19,400	15,951	−18%
Moderate Income Units			
$400 to $499	3,576	7,843	+119%
$500 to $599	1,833	5,556	+203%
Total	5,409	13,399	+148%
Upper Middle Income & Luxury Units			
$600 to $749	1,450	5,176	+257%
$750 to $999	2,261	4,642	+105%
$1,000 >	1,318	3,831	+191%
Total	5,029	13,640	+171%

New Yorkers found renting below this so-called reasonable threshold difficult, if not impossible. This issue proved even more difficult for low-income families, for whom allocating the majority of their income to rent was a fact of life. Nationwide in 1985, more than 79% of low-income renters paid 35% or more of their monthly income towards housing, and 55% paid more than 60% and teetered on the brink of homelessness.[11]

Contributing Factors

Beyond these structural causes, additional factors fueled the dramatic growth of the shelter population. In the 1980s, crack cocaine emerged as the drug of choice in New York's low-income neighborhoods, and Acquired Immune Deficiency Syndrome (AIDS) became a rampant threat for intravenous drug users.

It is difficult to identify a single reason that rendered families homeless; often it was a combination of factors. In many cases, drug addiction, domestic violence, and medical problems had a simultaneous and deleterious impact on families. In the downward spiral of poverty, cuts in social services, a lack of affordable housing, and larger economic trends only exacerbated pre-existing conditions. Without housing and employment solutions, families became the new clients of an over-stretched New York City shelter system.

The Emergency Shelter Build-up

In the city's scramble to provide shelter services, early efforts focused on short-term emergency assistance rather than the need for more affordable housing, social services, or preventative strategies. The situation grew so frantic that some shelter officials referred to long-range planning as "what will we do with these homeless families tomorrow night."[12] In perhaps a case study in poor planning, the city's main initiative simply provided shelter clients with a bed and a meal. While this was a reasonable response given the political and economic realities of the time, it did little to address the root causes of the problem.

The city's first line of defense simply continued a policy started in the 1970s that placed homeless families in vacant hotel rooms when shelter space ran out.[13] In 1983, the city began placing clients in hotels outside of New York City in Westchester County, Long Island, and New Jersey. Over three hundred families were placed in hotels in Secaucus, Union City, and Newark, New Jersey, alone. This action created tense inter-state relations between New York and New Jersey, and led New Jersey Governor Thomas Kean to decry the policy as "the height of irresponsibility."[14] In response, the city used readily available local facilities, such as gymnasiums and auditoriums, to create large congregate family shelters. Rows of metal sleeping cots filled these barracks-style locations based on the assumption that each family might only stay for two or three days. Yet not only did homeless families stay much longer, these congregate shelters became far more chaotic and unsafe than anyone imagined.[15]

The most infamous example was the two hundred and ten bed Roberto Clemente facility, opened in 1983 and located in a gymnasium on the grounds of the Roberto Clemente State Park in the Bronx. Privacy was non-existent: families had no secure place to leave their belongings, bathrooms were communal, and the lights remained on all night. Criticism of this shelter came from all sides. Community members and state officials complained that they could no longer utilize a part of this state park, homeless advocates objected to the shelter's overcrowded conditions, and city officials called the $70,000 per family annual cost outrageous.[16]

Responses from the Public and the Courts

At the same time that New Yorkers learned of conditions at congregate shelters like Roberto Clemente, the rest of America grew increasingly aware of the homeless epidemic. Numerous articles and media reports chronicled the plight of people living on steam grates and park benches, and the word "homeless" was coined to describe this new population—a more sensitive term than the earlier monikers of "tramp," "bum," and "hobo."[17] Interestingly, New York's growing shelter infrastructure fueled the misconception that homeless individuals from outside the region came to the city just to take advantage of its emergency shelter services.

There was also confusion over the less visible problem of homeless families. As parents and children tended to go to city shelters, rather than sleep on park benches on the streets, their situations were somewhat hidden and thus non-existent to the public. As a result, most people did not know that a homeless person could also be a child. In contrast, the public seemed well aware—and highly critical of—the large numbers of single mothers receiving welfare benefits. (Over 740,000 women received AFDC in New York City in 1984.) The popular press portrayed these women as "welfare queens," lazy women breeding babies in pursuit of the next welfare check.[18] In reality, of course, these were young women with young children, caught in the vicious cycle of poverty, for whom having children was frequently an unplanned by-product of their environment. Nonetheless, young, poor, single mothers received more condemnation than compassion in the press.

A small group of advocates, however, recognized the rights of these families and sued the city for the right to shelter for the homeless. Throughout the 1980s, the pro-bono lawyers of the Legal Aid Society sparred with city officials in a series of court battles. Labeling conditions at city intake centers and shelters inhumane, these advocates monitored the treatment of individual homeless families and filed legal petitions on their behalf. City officials grumbled in response that constant battles with Legal Aid created bureaucratic red tape and prevented them from implementing real reforms.

Ultimately, the Legal Aid Society won a series of court victories that made significant changes in city shelter regulations and established New York's right to shelter laws. In 1981, *Callahan v. Carey* affirmed the city's obligations to shelter single men and established minimum health and safety standards for shelters. The same right extended to homeless women a year later in *Eldredge v. Koch*. In 1986, the *McCain v. Koch* decision gave the right to shelter to homeless families with children and prohibited the city from allowing families to remain overnight in welfare offices.[19] Together, these rulings made great strides in improving conditions for homeless New Yorkers and guaranteed them the right to shelter, a mandate unique among urban areas. The chronological order of the court decisions also demonstrated the widespread public perception of homelessness. Men, the most visible segment of the population, were granted the right to shelter first, followed by women, and finally families, who were hidden away from public view and consequently not given much consideration.

The continuing growth of homelessness, the ensuing emergency responses, and the legal fights of the 1980s together laid the groundwork for today's shelter infrastructure. Through legal and political efforts New York City shelters evolved into a system unmatched by any other American city (most of which rely on private charities to provide shelter). Today, New York allocates $844 million to homeless services annually, with approximately $433 million allocated for families alone.[20] Nonetheless, the city's emergency efforts, band-aid solutions, and knee-jerk legal positions only exacerbated a growing problem.

Notes

[1] New York City Mayor's Office of Operations, *Mayor's Management Report* (New York: City of New York, 1985), 505. Subsequently, all volumes of this annual report will be referred to as *Mayor's Management Report* or *Mayor's Preliminary Management Report*.

2 *Mayor's Management Report,* 1988, 535.

3 L. Mishel, J. Bernstein, and J. Schmitt, *The State of Working America: 1998–1999* (Washington, DC: Economic Policy Institute, 1999), 208. Available at: http://www.epi.org

4 Ibid., 208.

5 Michael Stegman, *Housing and Vacancy Report: New York City* (New York: Department of Housing, Preservation, and Development, 1987).

6 Annie E. Casey Foundation, "KIDS COUNT Data Book," http://www.aecf.org.

7 Martha Burt, *Over the Edge: The Growth of Homelessness in the 1980s* (New York: Russell Sage Foundation, 1992) 83–87; Robert B. Reich, "As the World Turns," *The New Republic,* May 1, 1989, 28; Lisa Klee Mihaly, *Homeless Families: Failed Policies and Young Victims* (Washington, DC: Children's Defense Fund, January 1991), 14; Sylvia Ann Hewlett, *When the Bough Breaks: The Cost of Neglecting Our Children* (New York: Basic Books, 1991), 45, 148.

8 National Jobs With Peace Campaign, *Fact Sheet* (Boston: National Jobs With Peace Campaign, 1990) as cited in Padraig O'Malley, *Homelessness: New England and Beyond* (Amherst, MA: John W. McCormack Institute of Public Affairs, 1992).

9 National Low Income Housing Coalition, *Changing Priorities: The Federal Budget and Housing Assistance 1976–2007* (Washington, D.C.: National Low Income Hosing Coalition, 1990), 10.

10 Stegman, *Housing and Vacancy Report: New York City.*

11 Paul H. Leonard, Cushing N. Dolbeare, Edward B. Lazare, *A Place to Call Home: The Crisis in Housing for the Poor* (Washington, D.C.: National Low Income Housing Coalition, 1990), 10.

12 Larry Schatt, former Assistant Commissioner of Homeless Services, personal interview, 8 February 2002.

13 Kenneth Murphy, former Deputy Commissioner of Homeless Services, personal interview, 26 February 2002.

14 *Mayor's Management Report,* 1983, 440; "Cuomo Makes Visit to Homeless," *New York Times,* 19 December 1985.

15 Kenneth Murphy, personal interview.

16 Crystal Nix, "Housing Family in a Shelter Costs the City $70,000 Per Year," *New York Times,* 7 March 1986.

17 See Kenneth L. Kusmer, *Down and Out, On The Road: The Homeless In American History* (New York: Oxford University Press, 2002) for a further exploration of the various monikers for homeless individuals.

18 David Zucchino, *The Myth of the Welfare Queen* (New York: Simon and Schuster, 1997), 65. According to David Zucchino, Ronald Reagan helped bring the term into popular consciousness during his 1976 presidential campaign. Reagan mentioned in a speech that a Chicago welfare mother had allegedly cheated the system which gave her a "tax-free income" of "over $150,000." Newspapers reporting the story dubbed her the "welfare queen."

19 Coalition for the Homeless, *Right to Shelter for Homeless New Yorkers: Twenty Years and Counting* (New York: Coalition for the Homeless, June 2002). *Callahan v. Carey* was filed as a class action lawsuit in 1979. In 1981, it was settled as a court consent decree guaranteeing a right to shelter for homeless men in New York City,

and establishing minimum health and safety standards for shelters. *Eldredge v. Koch* was filed in 1982 and argued for equal rights and standards for homeless women. The case was eventually included in the *Callahan* decree and extended the right to shelter to women. *McCain v. Koch* was filed in 1986 on behalf of homeless families with children. The city was ordered to provide emergency housing to homeless families with children, and was prohibited from leaving families to remain overnight in welfare offices by the Appellate Division of the State Supreme Court. *McCain* extended the right to shelter homeless families with children. In 1990, *McCain* was amended, stipulating that the city must phase out the use of noncompliant welfare hotels and overnight shelter beds, provide permanent housing units for homeless families with children, and operate a 24-hour emergency intake center for homeless families. For more information, visit http://www.coalitionforthehomelesss.org.

[20] New York City *Preliminary Mayor's Management Report 2009*. According to the Independent Budget Office, FY2008 spending for the family shelter was budgeted at $433 million. See IBO News Fax # 157 "Inside the Budget—Has the Rise in Homeless Prevention Spending Decreased the Shelter Population?" 7 August 2008, 3.

2 The Mid-1980s
Emergency Efforts: The EAU and Welfare Hotels

The series of court decrees in the early eighties that guaranteed the right to shelter for every man, woman, and child in New York City put enormous pressure on city officials to deal with the growing homeless crisis. This resulted in the hasty implementation of quick-fix solutions and short-term policies. At the same time, in order to deter other poorly housed families from entering the shelter system, officials kept temporary shelter arrangements from becoming attractive alternatives. This strategy resulted in a costly shelter infrastructure with deteriorating facilities ill equipped to meet the needs of thousands of infants and young children.

Emergency Assistance Units

A family's journey through the shelter system began with intake, either at the local welfare office, known as Income Maintenance Centers (IMs) or, in the evening, at Emergency Assistance Units (EAUs). The EAUs, a unique concept at the time, were four intake offices where families could register and receive referrals to short-term shelter.[1] In reality, the EAUs functioned as overcrowded, chaotic holding pens, where families would wait for an initial conditional shelter placement for anywhere from four to twenty hours. Even after an assignment, many families endured multiple back-and-forth trips between an EAU and temporary shelter, all on a few hours of sleep. Before *McCain v. Koch* prohibited the practice, families unable to secure a placement before nightfall often spent the night sleeping on the floors of these centers.[2]

The EAUs were part of a system plagued by troubles from the very start. The city's homeless system's early years of operation lacked a comprehensive database to track placements or criteria to determine eligibility. Anyone claiming homelessness was entitled to shelter, regardless of income level or housing need. As a result, the EAUs suffered a near-constant backlog and instances of fraud. Occasionally, a family with an alternative living situation simply wanted a private hotel room for the weekend. Others intentionally entered the system just to get their names on the public housing waiting list, as homeless families received priority placements.[3] In sum, the EAUs did not work very well.

Tier I Facilities

In 1986, as EAU operations reorganized, New York State formalized a set of shelter regulations to ensure uniform safety standards and services. Shelters were categorized, with large congregate sites like Roberto Clemente classified as Tier I facilities. These congregate Tier I sites represented the least desirable housing option for homeless families, who commonly refused placements there.

City leaders actually hoped that the unappealing conditions at congregate facilities would serve as a deterrent to families seeking to enter the system.[4] A New York City Council report in 1986 challenged such deterrence theories. The report concluded that the worst facilities had the longest length of stay, while those with better conditions and enhanced social services had greater success moving families to long-term affordable housing. The practice of maintaining low-level congregate facilities continued nonetheless.[5]

Some city officials shared the dislike homeless families had for these facilities. One mayoral report called congregate shelters "wasteful, ineffective, and inefficient."[6] Considering the cost of food, maintenance, and security, housing just one family in a Tier I facility could cost as much as $145 per night.[7] Despite the high cost of sheltering families, these large shelters did not include comprehensive social services or housing search assistance. The city eventually began to scale back congregate placements. By the end of 1986, just 8% of the homeless family population, roughly 330 families, resided in Tier I sites (see Figure 5).[8]

Figure 5
Percent of Families Placed by Type of Shelter (New York City, 1986)
Source: *Mayor's Management Report,* 1986

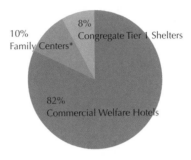

8%
Congregate Tier 1 Shelters

10%
Family Centers*

82%
Commercial Welfare Hotels

*A family center, later called a tier 2 facility, provides private/semi private accomodations as well as social services.

Welfare Hotels

By this time, 3,400 families, or 82% of the family population, lived in so-called commercial welfare hotels.[9] These hotels were a slight step up from congregate shelters but still substandard. They increasingly began to represent all the failings of the city's shelter policy and ultimately inspired public controversy in response.[10]

With little fanfare, the city began working on an adhoc basis with hotel owners willing to rent a couple of rooms, floors, or even an entire site to house homeless families. Such ventures were completely private, and managed by the hotel at a cost of up to $99 per room per night. Rates were determined individually with each site, averaging $53 per room, or $17 for the head of the household plus $12 for each additional family member.[11] The city defined one month's rent as 28 days in order to avoid a legal technicality (Local Law 4) that would give residents who stayed for more than 30 days the same anti-eviction rights as apartment tenants.[12] By 1986, the cost to house a family of four at a hotel for one year was estimated at nearly $20,000, not including food and services, and the city's total bill for such placements had climbed to $72 million annually.[13]

When families arrived at these hotels they found cramped, vermin-infested rooms, where narrow hallways and stairs were the only play areas available for their children. And despite their high price tag, these facilities offered neither the typical amenities of a hotel nor any supportive or educational services, with only one visiting social worker assigned to dozens of families.[14] The larger hotels, including the infamous Martinique and Holland hotels in Manhattan, quickly became hotbeds of criminal activity, with various "friends" and unwelcome "guests" using them as the base for thriving drug and prostitution rings. In this atmosphere, where anarchy reigned and security was minimal, safety became a concern for families with young children.

Hotel Scrutiny: The Media's Role

With the controversy over homeless hotels growing, newspapers began to expose some of the suspect practices of a chaotic and mismanaged system. At the time, the *New York Times* offices were across the street from the Hotel Carter in midtown Manhattan, a hotel the city itself openly criticized for its "consistently low rate of compliance in correcting health and safety violations."[15] The Holland Hotel, on West 42nd Street, was in turn cited for over a thousand health and building violations, including

Figure 6
Number of Families Residing in Commercial Welfare Hotels (New York City, 1984 to 1986)
Source: *Mayor's Management Report*, 1984 to 1986
1984 data includes families in congregate shelter as well as welfare hotels.

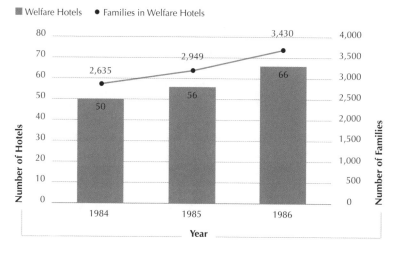

lack of hot water. The Environmental Control Board ultimately fined the hotel $40,000, on top of its $56,805 of unpaid water and sewer bills.[16] Nonetheless, the city continued to use such hotels to house homeless families (see Figure 6). Hotel owners reaped tremendous profits from the city. The owner of the Holland Hotel, for example, earned $6 million a year, $4 million of which came at the public's expense. Welfare hotels became so lucrative that many of the city's single room occupancy (SRO) buildings, which traditionally offered low-rent lodging for the poor, converted to hotels to turn greater profits.[17]

Ongoing publicity eventually revealed the tremendous hold that hotel proprietors had over city officials, who were under intense pressure to abide by the right to shelter regulations and house homeless families. The city had little control or negotiating power over the hotels, and the most basic of reforms met with resistance. For example, as rooms lacked kitchen facilities, the city provided each family with a restaurant allowance for food. Yet having a cold place to keep food, baby formula, and medicine was a necessity for mothers with young children, some of whom, out of desperation, stored baby bottles on windowsills. To address this, in 1985, the city attempted to give hotel families their own small refrigerators for nutritional and sanitary reasons.

The city's Human Resources Administration (HRA) purchased several hundred small refrigerators for mothers late in pregnancy or with newborns, but hotel managers refused to install the refrigerators unless the city relaxed its health inspections, to the end of reducing hotel violations. The city and the hotels reached a compromise wherein the city agreed to pay an extra fee, per room per week, to cover maintenance and replacement expenses. In the end, hotel operators fleeced the city in a series of economic shakedowns with families and children as pawns. Such sagas generated sympathy for homeless mothers and disgust for the hotel owners, who leveraged the issue to earn more money at the public's expense.

Eventually, media coverage led to the widespread realization that fifty-five welfare hotels comprised the city's homeless policy strategy. The public expressed outrage that the system wasted so much taxpayer money and simply "dumped" so many poor families on certain neighborhoods. Middle- and upper-class Manhattanites found this practice particularly threatening. Twenty-six percent of homeless families were concentrated in eight welfare hotels from Broadway to 3rd Avenue between 21st and 35th streets, traditionally one of Manhattan's more upscale neighborhoods.[18] Ultimately, it was this outcry that brought the first real reforms and forced the city to examine new policy avenues.

From Emergency to Long-term Solutions

The cost of sheltering homeless families grew exponentially; between 1978 and 1985, the city's budget allocation of aggregate state, local, and federal funds rose from $8 million to over $100 million.[19] The primary focus remained on "emergency" efforts because the administration believed that permanent housing efforts would encourage families to enter these shelter systems. With the tremendous controversies generated by emergency approaches like congregate shelter and welfare hotels, however, the Koch administration had no choice but to push for new residential options for homeless families.

Although the city did not have much land on which to build, it could boast ownership of thousands of empty buildings. By 1986, the city played landlord to 53,000 occupied units and 49,000 vacant ones obtained *in rem*—foreclosed on because of the non-payment of taxes.[20] In 1983, the Department of Housing Preservation and Development (HPD) had initiated a large-scale program to convert 4,474 *in rem* apartments into low-income housing for the homeless. Although this effort helped expand the supply of available units, it only renovated individual apartments and often left the building's shell, hallways and stairways in serious disrepair.

As a result, the Koch administration took a second look at the city's supply of *in rem* buildings and settled on a ten-year, $5.1 billion effort to build up New York City's reserve of permanent low-income housing for homeless families, a plan known as Housing New York.[21] Part of this effort included Koch's Special Initiatives Program (SIP): a four-year plan to completely rehabilitate 5,600 units of *in rem* housing into low-income apartments. This first wave of SIP would move 750 families from the ten largest hotels into affordable housing, but city officials soon discovered that the implementation of such a plan would take some time. Although change began, it would not be until the next mayoral administration that SIP housing became available, while the number of families entering the shelter system increased daily.[22]

The Move toward Transitional Housing

With the demand for apartments far exceeding the supply, homeless families languished in "short-term" shelters and hotels for an average of fourteen months.[23] Clearly, the system required a better residential model, one that could bridge the gap between homelessness and independent living. City officials and advocates alike contemplated a number of alternate approaches, including paying homeless families to double up with relatives, sending New York City's homeless families to live in vacant apartments throughout New York State, and even establishing mobile-home campgrounds throughout the five boroughs.[24]

The approach that officials ultimately considered the most cost-effective was the creation of "family centers," known as Tier II transitional facilities, operated by non-profit organizations. In the years to come, the city would vigorously pursue the development of these ventures, which would offer smaller, more home-like supportive living settings to help families move toward independence. Until recently, the operational success of Tier II shelters rendered them the dominant form of family shelter in the city.

Notes

[1] The EAU in Queens closed in 1993 and the Brooklyn location closed in 1994.

[2] Larry Schatt, personal interview, 8 February 2002.

[3] Ibid.

[4] Barbara Basler, "Koch Limits Using Welfare Hotels," *New York Times,* 17 December 1985.

[5] Jonathan Kozol, *Rachel and Her Children* (New York: Crown, 1988).

[6] New York City Commission on the Homeless, *The Way Home: A New Direction in Social Policy* (New York: New York City Commission on the Homeless, 1992), 13.

[7] New York City Commission on the Homeless, *The Way Home,* 110. The $145 per family per night is an estimate put forth by the New York City

Commission on the Homeless and is significantly less than the $70,000 per family per year mentioned earlier. The larger figure is specific to the Roberto Clemente shelter; the other refers to Tier Is in general.

8 *Mayor's Management Report, 1986.*

9 Ibid.

10 The notion of using hotels to handle the occasional nightly overflow of homeless families was not a new one for city officials. In 1971, the administration of then-Mayor John Lindsay placed a homeless family in the exclusive Waldorf-Astoria hotel for $77 per night, an experiment promptly abandoned following a media outcry over such an outrageous expense; Clara Hemphill, "The High Price of Sheltering City's Homeless," *Newsday,* 2 December 1988.

11 Manhattan Borough President's Task Force on Housing for Homeless Families, A *Shelter Is Not a Home* (New York: Manhattan Borough President's Task Force on Housing for Homeless Families, March 1987), 26.

12 According to Local Law #4.

13 Manhattan Borough President's Task Force on Housing for Homeless Families, A *Shelter Is Not a Home,* 26. Not including food and services, the direct shelter cost in 1986 was $19,716 annually at the Martinique Hotel and $21,900 at the Allerton Hotel.

14 Ibid., 115. According to this report, there was one caseworker for every sixty families.

15 Michael Goodwin, "State is Penalizing City Over Shelter Conditions," *New York Times,* 21 December 1983.

16 Barbara Basler, "Welfare Hotels Sued Over Taxes," *New York Times,* 27 December 1985.

17 Crystal Nix, "Profits of Welfare Hotels Placed at $3 Million," *New York Times,* 23 November 1985.

18 "New York Barred from Placing Needy Families in Midtown Hotels," Associated Press, 21 December 1986.

19 Ralph da Costa Nunez, *The New Poverty: Homeless Families in America* (New York: Insight Books, 1996), 34.

20 *In rem* is a legal term referring to an action or judgment against a property. In 1976, the city began foreclosing properties that were one year in tax arrears, in contrast to an earlier policy that allowed for a three-year grace period. The result was a sharp increase in the number of foreclosed and abandoned properties in the late 1970s. Housing First! "The Housing New York Ten-Year Plan." Available at: http://www.housingfirst.net/policypaper_app_b.html. Accessed for first publication.

21 Laura Castro, "Bankers Trust Funds Housing for Homeless," *Newsday,* 19 August 1990.

22 Thomas Lueck, "Breaking Ground in Housing Policy," *New York Times,* 30 April 1989.

23 Manhattan Borough President's Task Force on Housing for Homeless Families, A *Shelter Is Not a Home,* 2.

24 Michael Goodwin, "Carol Bellamy Fights Sharing of Apartments of Homeless Families," *New York Times,* 29 June 1984.

The Late 1980s and Early 1990s

Old Problems, New Strategies

The late eighties and early nineties marked a period of transition in New York City homeless policy. David Dinkins assumed the role of mayor, and the homeless services delivery system evolved and created a new city agency: the Department of Homeless Services (DHS).

By 1987, the number of homeless families in the shelter system had grown to roughly 5,000 (and would increase to almost 5,700 by 1993) (see Figure 7).[1] Each year, the Emergency Assistance Units (EAUs) grew more crowded, with families waiting all day and through the night for placement (see Figure 8). Every evening, officials performed frantic

Figure 7
Average Daily Family Shelter Census (New York City, 1987 to 1993)
Source: *Mayor's Management Report*, 1987 to 1993

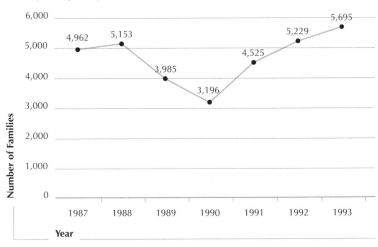

Figure 8

Average Families Seen Per Night at Emergency Assistance Units
(New York City, 1987 to 1993)
Source: *Mayor's Management Report*, 1987 to 1993

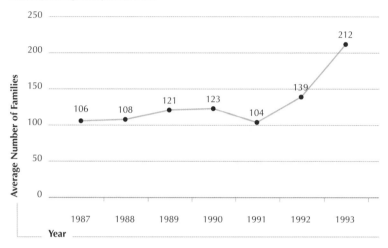

searches to find available hotel rooms, apartments, or shelter slots, often of questionable quality.[2]

Both mayors Ed Koch and David Dinkins shared a commitment to helping homeless families. When Koch held office, the crisis was so nascent that his administration simply centered on providing emergency beds. By the Dinkins era, the focus had moved away from congregate shelters and welfare hotels towards transitional Tier II facilities and, ultimately, permanent low-income housing.

Mayor Dinkins pursued this strategy in part to fulfill his campaign promise of putting welfare hotels out of business. In 1989, 1,500 families lived in these hotels; by 1990, the number was down to 150.[3] The goal of "zero day," when no homeless families would reside in hotels, seemed well within reach (see Figure 9).[4] The continual rise of incoming families, however, blunted this success and by 1992, the number of families living in hotels grew to over one thousand.[5]

Figure 9
Distribution of Families in Temporary Housing (New York City, 1987 to 1992)
Source: *Mayor's Management Reports,* 1987 to 1992

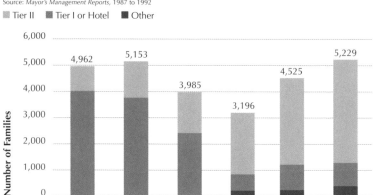

A New Agency

In his efforts to confront the crisis in a meaningful way, Mayor Dinkins created a Blue Ribbon Commission on Homelessness in 1992 to evaluate the city's existing shelter system and to come up with new ways to improve homeless policy. An assemblage of city officials, public policy experts, homeless advocates, and non-profit administrators met for six months and issued a series of recommendations in the report "The Way Home: A New Direction in Social Policy." The commission called for the contracting of transitional housing to non-profit service providers and the development of more small service-rich transitional facilities. It also proposed the creation of an entirely new agency, responsible for the implementation of the commission's recommendations and the operation and oversight of all homeless services.[6] The newly-established Department of Homeless Services (DHS) absorbed the agency for Adult and Family Services and the Mayor's Office of Homeless Services (established by Koch in 1986). In 1993, DHS began to assume responsibility for the city's homeless from the Human Resources Administration (HRA) and took over shelter provision services for homeless families and individuals, and the development of citywide homeless policy.[7]

Transitioning to Tier II

The recommendations from the Dinkins report confirmed what many advocates and city officials had long understood: the shelter system desperately needed reform. Emergency shelter and welfare hotels were costly, dangerous, and doing little to help families escape poverty. Even after families finally left the shelter system for a housing placement, their reprieve from homelessness was often short-lived. A 1992 study by the city Department of Housing Preservation and Development (HPD) found a high recidivism rate within the homeless population, with half of all the families reapplying for housing after having received a placement on a prior occasion.[8] Any new shelter initiative would have to target the challenges homeless families faced in living stable, independent lives.

As was frequently the case with homeless policy during this era, the courts initiated change. A 1990 consent order decree in the *McCain* v. *Koch* decision outlawed the use of welfare hotels and congregate Tier I shelters for families, leading the City Council to mandate the closing of all Tier I sites by 1991.[9] In response, the city began the frantic process of converting hospitals, schools, and other facilities into Tier II shelters, as well as designing and building new ones. The continued rise in the number of new homeless families prevented the city from meeting its goal of closing all Tier I shelters until 1993.[10]

Tier I shelters were no longer the first stop on the road to shelter, but city officials could not ensure that every family received a Tier II placement, a problem that remains today. Still, by 1994, 70% of the city's homeless families had moved into Tier II units, at a cost of roughly $33 per person per day, compared to $145 per family per day in a Tier I site.[11]

As city officials focused more on policy and regulations than shelter operations, they called upon the non-profit sector to design and operate the Tier II system. At the time, non-profit shelter operators were permitted to selectively admit clients into their facilities. Consequently, some city administrators objected to awarding non-profit shelter operators' contracts, and charged that they achieved favorable outcomes by selecting the most promising families from the pool of homeless applicants, a process known as creaming. HRA in particular argued that non-profit transitional housing operators creamed the smallest, least troubled families, leaving the city to deal with the "problem" cases.[12]

Despite these charges, experience demonstrated that these organizations could provide technical expertise and efficient services without a complicated bureaucracy or a high price tag. As a result the city began to withdraw from direct service provision and by the late 1980s, the private non-profit groups became the primary service providers. These organizations would further develop the Tier II model in response to the needs of homeless families and influence the evolution of homeless policy in New York.

With different providers managing different types of facilities, the first transitional shelters had varied features, including communal kitchens, bathrooms, or living areas. By the late 1980s, the definition of a transitional city facility grew uniform, with the State's Part 900 regulations governing what a "Tier II" shelter looked like. According to these regulations, Tier II family shelters were facilities that provided shelter and services to ten or more homeless families. These facilities offered, at a minimum, private rooms, three meals a day, childcare, health services, assessment and referral to services, and guidance in the permanent housing placement process. The regulations also set the average length of stay for families in shelter at six months. In reality, families would stay significantly longer.[13]

Local Resistance: Not in My Backyard

In the move toward transitional housing, city administration and non-profit providers encountered strong resistance from neighborhood groups. Tier I shelters operated in empty armories, old schools, and welfare hotels; Tier II housing was meant to span existing neighborhoods in all five boroughs. This new housing system required both physical construction and mental flexibility, as local residents might come to know the homeless as the people next door. Not surprisingly, people responded with a "not in my backyard" (NIMBY) attitude, while community boards and neighborhood associations waged opposition against proposed facilities and argued that Tier II shelters would lower property values. Lawsuits backed by local politicians, coupled with intense media coverage, became stumbling blocks in the campaign to build or rehabilitate new transitional housing.

Despite local opposition, by 1988, the city boasted thirty-three Tier II family centers, up from only four in 1986 (see Figure 10).[14] These facilities mirrored similar models in supervised housing for youth, the mentally ill, and the elderly and proved successful models of transitional, non-profit operated housing. More homelike than congregate shelters, but with more supervision and services than private apartments and housing projects, Tier II shelters helped families build a foundation to move toward independent living.

Figure 10
Number of Tier II Family Centers (New York City, 1984 to 1988)
Source: *Mayor's Management Report,* 1984 to 1988

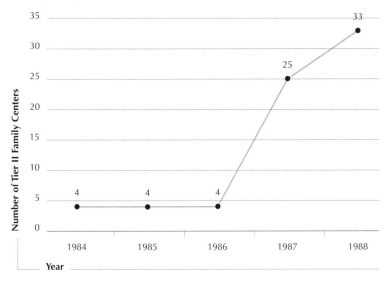

Steps Forward, Steps Back

The architects of the Tier II shelter system designed it with the understanding that these shelters could convert to permanent housing once the homeless crisis was over. By the early 1990s, the situation was nowhere near its end and despite efforts to build more permanent housing, the supply of new affordable units could not meet demands.

Initially, the Dinkins administration seemed to make strides in housing families. This was, in part, because five thousand units of Koch's 1986–1990 Special Initiatives Program (SIP) came on-line and the wait for permanent housing went from eighteen to twenty-four months in 1987 to only three to six months in 1990.[15] Dinkins also made changes to the Emergency Assistance Rehousing Program (EARP) to facilitate permanent placements. Begun in 1983, EARP paid stipends and bonuses to private landlords who housed homeless families. For ten years, the program was generally ineffective until Dinkins enhanced it with supplemental federal Section 8 rental vouchers.[16] The vouchers helped families pay the difference between 30% of their income and the fair market rent. As part of this new EARP/Section 8 initiative, the city paid for a family's moving expenses, broker's fees, security deposits, and furniture, and landlords received cash bonuses (see Figure 11).[17] As a result of Dinkins' changes, the number of families living in EARP apartments went from 721 in 1990 to 2,227 in 1993 (see Figure 12).

Figure 11
One-time EARP Bonus by Number of Family Members
Source: New York City Department of Homeless Services

Figure 12

Number of Families Placed in Permanent Housing by Category (New York City, 1990 and 1993)

Source: New York City Department of Homeless Services

■ 1990   ■ 1993

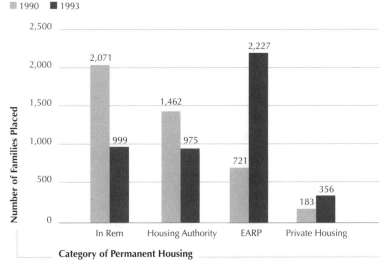

Although Dinkins' camp could point to the success of both SIP and EARP, these programs could not keep pace with the growing number of homeless apartment seekers. EARP in particular faltered as the flourishing private rental market of the 1990s allowed many private landlords to reject the program — no bonus could make it financially attractive to owners to pass up a private tenant who was willing and able to pay higher rent.

With these challenges, the administration pursued a delicate balancing act between supplying enough housing and preventing additional families from entering the system. When a family entered the shelter system, it was automatically prioritized on the city's subsidized housing list and displaced other poor but non-homeless individuals who might have been waiting for years for available slots.[18] Shelter providers who sought to place their clients in public housing projects met resistance from the city's Housing Authority (NYCHA), which was reluctant to receive "problem families" as tenants when there was a long waiting list of qualified non-homeless persons. In response to such issues, the city scaled back these homeless prioritizations.

Emergency Assistance: The Federal Approach

Throughout the 1980s and early 1990s, the federal government fought the homeless battle as well. The first large-scale federal aid programs included the Department of Agriculture's Temporary Food Assistance Program, Health and Human Services' Emergency Assistance Program, and Housing and Urban Development's Community Development Block Grants. In 1987, the McKinney Assistance Act, the first, largest, and only major federal homeless funding initiative, overshadowed these earlier efforts.

The act, originally called the Homeless Persons' Survival Act, was introduced in Congress in 1986 and contained emergency relief, preventive measures, and long-term solutions to homelessness. After the death of its chief sponsor, it assumed the title of the Stewart B. McKinney Homeless Assistance Act. President Ronald Reagan signed the bill into law in 1987. Upon its enactment, the McKinney legislation consisted of fifteen programs including: emergency shelter, transitional housing, job training, primary health care, education, and some permanent housing. Although the legislation received just over $1 billion in authorized funds for 1987 and 1988, a total of only $712 million was actually appropriated.[19]

In 1990, Congress amended the McKinney Act after receiving new information that homeless children faced serious educational obstacles. The new amendments detailed the obligation of the states to provide homeless children and youth with access to public education and revise policies that might act as a barrier to academic success.[20] Despite McKinney's significance, its programs suffer from insufficient funding. Critics also charge that the legislation focuses too heavily on emergency measures and thus ignores the root causes of homelessness. For example, in 1993, 78% of the appropriated funding went to food and shelter while only 5% was allocated for education and job training (see Figure 13). Nonetheless, the McKinney Act remains landmark legislation.[21]

New Directions: Tightening the Door

Most everyone agreed that children were the main victims of the rising tide of family homelessness. Whether their parents were equally innocent

Figure 13
Allocation of McKinney Act Funding (1993)
Source: U.S. General Accounting Office, 1993

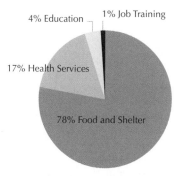

4% Education   1% Job Training

17% Health Services

78% Food and Shelter

was a matter of increasing debate. Some actually speculated that city policies had the effect of enticing not-yet-homeless "welfare queens" to join the shelter rolls.

There also existed questions of eligibility. Did families really need shelter, or did the shelter system simply offer a fast-track to an apartment? Social workers voiced concern about educational, mental, and health problems among shelter residents that could hinder successful independent living. Public opinion of homeless adults grew increasingly negative; they were widely perceived as drug addicts and alcoholics taking advantage of the system.

In the decade to come, Mayor Rudolph Giuliani and his administration would tackle these issues with a "tight front door" policy that screened homeless families more carefully to determine their level of need. At the same time, sweeping policy changes on the national level ushered in an era of welfare reform with consequences that would have a significant impact on homelessness, and homeless families in particular.

Notes

[1] *Mayor's Management Report*, 1987 to 1993.

[2] Officials at the Emergency Assistance Unit dubbed Friday night "couples night" because so many couples would come to the intake center seeking shelter. These men and women would show up after-hours, when the EAU no longer had

access to Tier II facilities, knowing instead they would be placed in a hotel. After spending the weekend in the hotel, many couples would disappear, only to return again the following week. Larry Schatt, personal interview, 8 February 2002.

[3] New York City Commission on the Homeless, *The Way Home: A New Direction in Social Policy* (New York: New York City Commission on the Homeless, 1992), 73.

[4] Schatt, personal interview.

[5] *Mayor's Management Report, 1993*, 424.

[6] New York City Commission on the Homeless, *The Way Home*, 17.

[7] *Mayor's Management Report, 1993*, 402, 465; *Mayor's Management Report, 1994*, 263.

[8] New York City Commission on the Homeless, *The Way Home*, 72.

[9] Ibid.

[10] *Mayor's Management Report 1993*, 429.

[11] New York City Commission on the Homeless, *The Way Home*, 72.

[12] Manhattan Borough President's Task Force on Housing for Homeless Families, *A Shelter Is Not a Home* (New York: Manhattan Borough President's Task Force on Housing for Homeless Families, 1987), 122.

[13] Tier II shelter regulations are encoded in the Part 900 Regulations of Title 18 of *New York State Codes, Rules and Regulations*.

[14] New York City Department of Homeless Services, *Family Services Fact Sheet for Fiscal Year 2000*, http://www.nyc.gov/htm/dhs/fs-factsheets.html.

[15] Schatt, personal interview.

[16] Heather Haddon, "City Homeless Program Rewards Bad Landlords," *Norwood News*, 4 December 2002.

[17] The EARP program is the city's largest re-housing program, and is administered by the Department of Homeless Services in conjunction with the New York City Housing Authority.

[18] Schatt, personal interview.

[19] National Coalition for the Homeless, *National Coalition for the Homeless Fact Sheet #18: The McKinney Act*, April 1999.

[20] Project Hope, "History of the McKinney Act," http://www.wm.edu/education/ HOPE/national/mckinney/mckinney.html. Accessed for first publication.

[21] National Coalition for the Homeless, *National Coalition for the Homeless Fact Sheet #18*.

4 The Mid-1990s

Getting Tough: A New Administration's Approach

Mayor Rudolph Giuliani's singular vision in large measure defined New York City homeless policy during the mid-1990s. At a time when many saw the city as unmanageable and out of control, Giuliani sought to prove the opposite by prosecuting both major and minor crimes. The mayor believed that attention to petty offenses reduced all levels of crime and social problems. During his eight-year tenure, which commenced in 1994, Giuliani pursued "quality of life" campaigns; one such effort was to rid the city of the homeless by prosecuting squeegee car washers and subway panhandlers.

The administration's drive for efficiency and order led to an overhaul in the delivery of welfare services, a cut in the city's housing development budget, and the transfer of many of the city's low-income housing units to private developers. Simultaneously, the depletion of affordable housing fueled an increase in the number of homeless families and demonstrated that Giuliani's get-tough regulatory approach to reform could not seamlessly fit the needs of homeless children and their parents.

National Context

The economic and political tides affecting the nation provided the impetus for many of the homeless policy decisions made by city officials at this time. In the early 1990s, the country experienced a crippling eight-month recession, with the jobless rate reaching 7.8% nationwide and 11% in New York City in 1992.[1] All told, 12.3 million workers lost their jobs between 1987 and 1991, and many of those jobs were permanent, long-term positions. When the recession ended, there was a lag before employment began to rise again, particularly in large urban areas like New York.

Despite the previous downturn, the United States emerged from the 1991 recession directly into an unprecedented ten-year economic boom. With the growth of the information technology sector and the proliferation of dot-com millionaires, many felt a new spirit of optimism and the sense that prosperity would triumph over poverty. In line with this thinking, the newly elected President Bill Clinton campaigned on the promise to "end welfare as we know it." Like many policy makers, Clinton recognized that the decades-old Aid for Families with Dependent Children (AFDC) welfare program demanded significant reform. Some states, such as Wisconsin and New York, started experimental programs that provided jobs to welfare recipients and met with modest success.

The federal government looked to expand such work-fare programs nationwide, and a Republican-controlled Congress took President Clinton's pledge to "end welfare" to heart and drafted the "Contract with America," and the Personal Responsibility and Work Opportunity Act. Signed into law in 1996, the new law replaced AFDC with Temporary Assistance for Needy Families (TANF), effectively ending a lifetime of aid, enacting new work requirements, and providing large block grants to the states with broad responsibilities for creating new work-fare programs.

Supporters of the law, including New York's Republican mayor, charged that AFDC created a class of habitual benefits abusers, encouraged fraud and laziness, and locked generations into a cycle of poverty. They cited the staggering number of welfare recipients as evidence: in 1995, one in every eight New Yorkers received welfare benefits, a total of 1.1 million people in New York City alone.[2]

The new bill was far more stringent than Clinton and his fellow Democrats had envisioned. It gave recipients a five-year lifetime limit to receive benefits and a two-year deadline to find employment, although states had the flexibility to increase the lifetime limit through state-level welfare extension programs. New York, for example, established the Safety Net Assistance Program because of its state constitutional requirement to provide for the needy.[3] Regardless of such provisions, the rules of the game had been changed.

City Welfare Reforms

The national legislation gave New York officials the permission to develop new reform initiatives while tightening welfare eligibility rules. The state's two major welfare programs, AFDC and Home Relief, became Family Assistance and Safety Net Assistance, respectively. The most significant changes occurred at the city level, where local, rather than state, agencies administer welfare programs.

In the midst of sweeping changes at the national and state levels, city leaders took the opportunity to overhaul services for the poor. Local officials now followed Mayor Giuliani's mandate: "The real meaning of compassion" is to help "people make the transition from dependency on government to a life of self sufficiency."[4] In practice, this policy translated into more bureaucratic hurdles, including stricter rules and stiffer penalties, for those in need of services.

The Mayor's attempt to "close the front door" by creating roadblocks to government aid lent itself not only to homeless policies, but also to the city's entire approach to poverty and government assistance. These efforts took shape in two of the city's most controversial programs: the Job Centers and Work Experience Program (WEP). The Job Centers were a revision of the city's welfare offices, or income maintenance centers, which traditionally administered benefits for clients. Though ostensibly in existence to help people find jobs, critics charged that Job Center visitors were frequently discouraged from applying for aid and disqualified from employment programs. The Work Experience Program was similarly contentious, as it required welfare recipients to participate in city work programs in exchange for benefits at a quarter of regular union pay, which made it impossible to earn a living wage.

The New Homeless Journey

At the same time that the Mayor restricted access to welfare benefits, he imposed a new hard line on the existing shelter system and created a number of roadblocks for shelter seekers. In one step forward, the Giuliani administration made the Department of Homeless Services (DHS) a permanent agency. Prior to 1999, DHS existed on a trial basis under a "sunset" clause. With the passage of Local Law 19, DHS became a permanent independent mayoral agency on May 18, 1999.[5] For the first time, all services for homeless persons consolidated under one authority. Yet, most of the administration's efforts on homelessness centered on countering the perception that many families used the system despite other alternatives. Special staff investigated an applying family's housing history to help them identify other options — from staying with relatives to finding an appropriate apartment referral service. As a direct result, the number of families denied shelter rose from 365 in 1995 to 14,041 in 1998 (see Figure 14).[6]

Figure 14
Homeless Families Denied Shelter (New York City, 1995 and 1998)
Source: Coalition for the Homeless

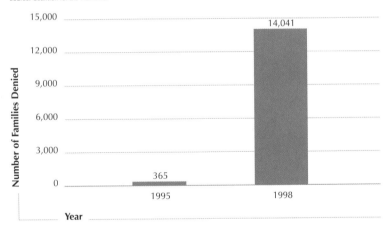

With the hope of limiting family intake, the Giuliani administration attempted to literally close the doors to the city's Emergency Assistance Units (EAUs). The Human Resources Administration had originally wanted to eliminate the use of the three EAUs in the outer boroughs by establishing one consolidated center in Manhattan. It was the Department of Homeless Services, however, that closed the Queens EAU in November 1993 and the Brooklyn EAU in January 1994. Unable to find an appropriate site for the consolidated facility, DHS ultimately closed the Manhattan EAU and extended the hours of the EAU in the Bronx to around the clock. Yet the administration persisted and attempted to eliminate the use of EAUs altogether by closing the one remaining Bronx facility and referring families to the Income Support Center or an after-hours hotline.[7]

Although the courts blocked this proposal, the administration remained convinced that "the existing shelter system had sent the perverse message to those who are poorly housed, that it is the only route to improving their living situations."[8] In turn, the city considered offering various incentives to keep people from entering the shelter system, from giving out bunk beds so that families could better double up, to providing subsidies for families opting to make their own living arrangements. Under these proposed reforms, families would remain in the homeless housing queue but not take up valuable shelter space.

Attacks on Low-income Housing

As Giuliani worked on closing the door to welfare programs and creating new hurdles in the shelter system, he also drastically reduced the city's potential supply of low-income housing by reforming the Department of Housing Preservation and Development (HPD). HPD had once overseen the transformation of city-owned, tax-foreclosed properties into affordable public housing stock, but now such properties rapidly sold to private owners (see Figure 15). At the same time that these building went to the private market, the administration espoused an active campaign to remove squatters from such abandoned city properties.

In 1995, Giuliani began the Building Blocks! Initiative, a program designed to create low-income cooperatives by returning city-owned *in rem* properties to "responsible private owners" such as landlords, private developers, non-profit groups, and tenant associations (see Figure 16).[9] Intended to stimulate community renewal, the initiative reduced city stock in *in rem* buildings to an all-time low in 1999.[10] While the Building Blocks! Program had good intentions, namely to create more community-

Figure 15
City-owned Vacant and Occupied Housing Units (New York City, 1994 to 2002)
Source: *NYC 2007 Housing Supply Report*, City-Owned Properties FY 1986–2006

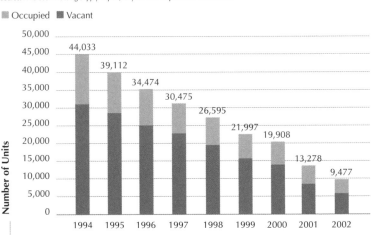

based affordable housing, the city placed no requirements on what private owners could do with the property.[11] Some poor families watched as low-income apartments in their neighborhood transformed into luxury housing, while others who had hoped for improvements upon local abandoned properties were left disappointed.

Similar threats to affordable housing occurred on the national level. Nationwide, over 27,600 federal low-income housing units had been demolished by the end of 1999. Despite the Department of Housing and Urban Development's replacement goal of 45%, only 7,273 units, or 26%, were replaced by the end of the year. Moreover, roughly 90,000 privately-owned subsidized rental units were also lost because landlords preferred to rent at market prices.[12]

Together, these events significantly reduced the supply of available-affordable housing. Although supplemental programs such as Emergency Assistance Rehousing Program (EARP) and Section 8 helped to bolster the stock of subsidized housing within the city, the success of such efforts rested with the willingness of landlords to accept Section 8 vouchers.

Figure 16
Building Blocks! Program: Housing Units Returned to Private Sector (New York City, 1996 to 2002)
Source: *Mayor's Management Report*, 1996 to 2002

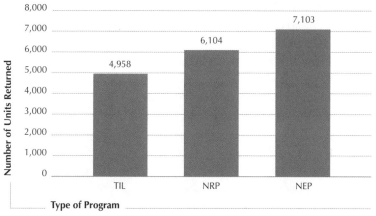

* Buildings sold through the Tenant Interim Program (TIL) are rehabilitated and then sold to existing residents as low-income cooperatives. The Neighborhood Redevelopment Program (NRP) represents buildings sold to non-profit organizations. Buildings sold through the Neighborhood Entrepreneurs Program (NEP) are sold to locally-based entrepreneurs.

In the end, many families—who often waited for upwards of eight years to receive a Section 8 subsidy—discovered that potential landlords found the private market more lucrative than subsidized participation.

More Controversy

In the late 1990s, a series of well-publicized incidents involving mentally ill homeless adults inspired an even tougher city stance on the homeless. Although families constituted a very different population than such high-profile offenders as Larry Hogue, the "wild man of 96th Street," and Paris Drake, "the Midtown brick thrower," the word homeless began to have a criminal connotation.[13]

In 1999, city officials responded to public concerns by enforcing stricter shelter rules first issued by Mayor Giuliani and Governor George Pataki in 1994. The regulations permitted the expulsion of homeless residents from city shelters for a thirty-day period if they violated shelter rules, failed to comply with an assessment or service plan, or ignored public assistance regulations. Mayor Giuliani took the regulations a step further by proposing that all shelter residents work, or else lose their shelter placement and potentially their children to foster care. In sum, if a client refused to comply, he or she would face ejection from the shelter system. This would perhaps render a client unable to care for his or her child. With a child's well-being in question, the city could intervene yet again and place the child in foster care.

During the Mayor's brief senate run against Hillary Rodham Clinton in 2000, these shelter rules became a major campaign issue.[14] Opponents held rallies and signed petitions while Clinton denounced the policy of parent-child separation. In the same vein, nearly all of the city's non-profit-operated Tier II shelters pledged noncompliance with the new protocol. Ultimately, the courts found the policies unlawful, because they violated the terms of previous rulings guaranteeing the right to shelter, including the 1981 *Callahan* decree and subsequent decisions.

The flack over the shelter regulations, workfare, and foster care marked a significant turning point in public opinion about homelessness. Media reports, combined with New Yorkers' personal experiences with homeless people in their neighborhoods, resulted in the collective realization that the city's quality-of-life campaign was too aggressive in its prosecution of the homeless. Some New Yorkers may have viewed their neighborhood panhandler as a nuisance, but not as a felon. Moreover, individuals understood that a revolving door between jail, shelters, and the street did nothing to help mentally ill homeless adults improve their situations. Nonetheless, ever-adamant Mayor Giuliani continued to argue that "streets do not exist in civilized societies for the purpose of people sleeping there. Bedrooms are for sleeping."[15]

Reflections

Mayor Rudolph Giuliani incited more controversy for his decisions regarding poverty and homelessness than did any other New York City mayor. Towards the end of Giuliani's mayoral reign, many predicted he would make history as a crime-control tyrant who trampled on the rights of 23,000 homeless New Yorkers. The September 11th World Trade

Center tragedy changed that perception overnight. Many considered Giuliani's actions in the wake of the attack as both compassionate and heroic. By the time he left office on January 1, 2002, the post-9/11 revision of Giuliani overshadowed his pre-9/11 policies and their impact on his legacy.

The Mayor also garnered praise for his successful campaign against crime, a problem many believed no city government could solve. Giuliani's proactive measures to combat disorder, fraud, and urban blight responded directly to city residents who demanded a safer metropolis. Giuliani's supporters overlooked his more extreme policies and rationalized that they were a necessary part of experimental new tactics.

The eight tumultuous years between 1993 and 2001 marked the reversal of several positive policy developments previously won for homeless families. Despite the continued increase in the number of homeless families, Giuliani ignored the rising tide of poor families and called for increased individual responsibility. Rather than garnering sympathy, homelessness became criminally suspect. Yet hard-line tactics, like the "street-sweeps" that rounded up homeless men, ignored the circumstances of homeless children and families in the New York City shelter system. This population's numbers continued to grow, so that by the beginning of 2002, the typical homeless person in the city was a poor, minority child under the age of five.[16]

All told, the effects of the Giuliani administration's policy and national welfare reform forced New Yorkers of all political persuasions to re-examine which policy strategies might best help the homeless. As Mayor Giuliani left office, many expected his handpicked successor, wealthy Republican Michael Bloomberg, to continue his predecessor's draconian policies towards the poor. Instead, the new mayor brought an unexpected commitment and focus to the issue.

Notes

[1] National Bureau of Economic Research, Bureau of Labor Statistics, New York State Department of Labor, 1992.

[2] Mayor's Press Office, "Mayor Giuliani Opens Coney Island Job Center," Press Release #239–01, 5 July 2001.

[3] New York City Human Resources Administration, *Running Out of Time: The Impact of Federal Welfare Reform* (New York: Human Resources Administration), July 2001.

[4] Mayor's Press Office, "Mayor Giuliani Opens Coney Island Job Center."

[5] The New York City Department of Homeless Services, "About the Department," http://www.nyc.gov/html/dhs/html/aboutnycdhs.html.

[6] Coalition for the Homeless, *Preserve the Right to Shelter: History,* http://www.right2shelter.org/history.htm.

[7] *Mayor's Management Report,*1993, 403; *Mayor's Management Report,* 1994, 265.

[8] New York City Department of Homeless Services, *Reforming New York City's System of Homeless Services* (New York: New York City Department of Homeless Services, 1994) 2.

[9] New York City Department of Housing Preservation and Development, *HPD Announces New Round of Building Blocks!,* http://www.nyc.gov./html/hpd/html/archive/rfq1-pr.html.

[10] Ibid.

[11] Ta-Nehishi Coates, "Empty Promises: Housing Activists Say the City Wastes Its Vacant Lots," *The Village Voice,* 12 March 2003.

[12] Joint Center for Housing Studies, *The State of the Nation's Housing: 2000* (Cambridge: Harvard University, 2000).

[13] Larry Hogue, suffering from mental illness and an addiction to crack cocaine, terrorized East 96th Street in upper Manhattan during the early 1990s, vandalizing property and assaulting residents. He was in and out of jails and mental hospitals for years. Paris Drake, another mentally-ill substance abuser with more than two dozen jail stints on his record, struck a young woman with a brick in 1999 near Grand Central Station. The incident received considerable attention from media.

[14] "Homelessness Emerges as Campaign Issue for Clinton and Giuliani," CNN, 5 December 1999.

[15] Elisabeth Bumiller, "In Wake of Attack, Giuliani Cracks Down on Homeless," *New York Times,* 20 November 1999.

[16] "Homeless Shelters in NY Filled to the Highest Level Since '80s," *New York Times,* 17 January 2002.

The Late 1990s, 2000, and Beyond

Conflict and Consensus

The beginning of the new millennium brought a renewed focus to an old problem. In 2002, in the wake of the World Trade Center disaster and the onset of an economic downturn, Michael Bloomberg was elected mayor and homelessness was once again thrust into the forefront. With an overall shelter population increase of 25% between 2001 and 2002 alone, the city experienced the largest one-year rise in homelessness since the modern shelter system began in the early 1980s.[1] The number of homeless families increased from a little over five thousand in 2000 to over nine thousand in 2003, with average shelter stays lasting more than eleven months (see Figure 17).[2]

This influx of shelter seekers posed an enormous challenge to the new administration as it scrambled to meet the demand for new beds. In 2002 — and in violation of the court order prohibiting the practice of sleeping on the floor of the Emergency Assistance Unit (EAU) — an average of thirty people slept at the EAU on any given night. In the summer months, that average climbed to fifty people.[3] In response, top Bloomberg aides converted the former Bronx House of Detention into a temporary family shelter. The city erected partition walls and concealed barred windows so that the gloomy space would appear less foreboding.[4] Despite all efforts to make the old jail habitable, the move generated tremendous negative publicity for the city from both advocates and the media alike.[5]

In that same year, a troubled sixteen-year-old boy committed suicide in a city welfare hotel. According to his family, he took his own life after the city threatened to return them to the EAU.[6] These two events created the impression that Mayor Bloomberg was not sympathetic to homeless families. After all, even conservative Mayor Giuliani

Figure 17
Average Daily Family Shelter Census (New York City, 1998 to 2003)
Source: *Mayor's Management Report*, 2003

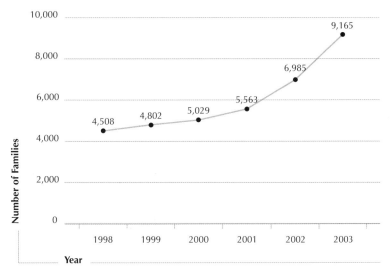

considered, but ultimately abandoned, the idea of turning jails into shelters. And how could the EAU have deteriorated so much under Bloomberg that a teenager would take his life rather than return there?

The public also criticized the administration for its stance on who should be guaranteed shelter and who should be punished for disregarding shelter rules. For single adults, the administration proposed revoking the right to shelter for up to 180 days for failure to comply with shelter service plans. For families, it unveiled the "Demonstration Project" permitting the city to place homeless children in foster care for thirty days if their parents turned down suitable apartments, arguing that some homeless parents repeatedly rejected worthy housing while holding on to much-needed shelter bed space. Ultimately, the city did not put either measure to use but the climate surrounding homeless policy during the first years of the Bloomberg administration nonetheless was one of economic downturn, an increasing demand for shelter, and severe criticism of both homeless policies and the decaying conditions of the EAU.

Change for the Better

Mayor Bloomberg also implemented some important and largely positive policy changes. In the winter of 2003, after twenty years of litigation with the Legal Aid Society, the city reached a historic legal settlement hailed as a victory for both homeless families and the city. The agreement stipulated that policy decisions on the homeless would no longer be made in a court of law. Instead, an independent three-member "special master panel" would mediate disputes among the city, homeless families, and advocates.

In addition to oversight and mediation, the panel was created to review the city's current policies and develop a long-term plan. All parties easily agreed on the panelists: John D. Feerick, an experienced mediator and former dean of the Fordham University School of Law; Daniel Kronenfeld, former director of the Henry Street Settlement with over thirty years of experience working with homeless families; and Gail B. Nayowith, executive director of the Citizens Committee for Children of New York. The monumental settlement ended the ongoing legal battles that have shaped city policy toward the homeless for the last several decades.

By 2004, the special master panel had made some important recommendations regarding the city's current policies and intake process. Perhaps one of the most significant was the "fundamental restructuring of the EAU into a Family Shelter Intake Center and a functional transformation of shelter application and eligibility processes to shift from a shelter-only system of care to one with a homelessness prevention focus where shelter is only one of the many housing-related services and supports offered to homeless families with children."[7] In November 2004, DHS opened a new intake facility for families with children, the Prevention Assistance and Temporary Housing (PATH) center. By the summer of 2005, all families applying for shelter went to the PATH center in the Bronx, and the EAU closed its doors.

The creation of the new PATH center intake ushered in significant changes in protocol: requests could only be made during business hours, with the intake process shortened to half a day; and both late-night shelter placements and overnights at the center were eliminated. DHS instituted a mid-application conference among clients, PATH's legal staff, and caseworkers to inform the applicant of any outstanding information germane to his or her case. The new process also introduced prevention and referral resources to assist ineligible applicants and ease their transition back to the community.[8]

A New Strategy: Census Control

At the same time that the city created the new intake center, it put forth a new plan to address homelessness. Largely in response to a nationwide trend of decade-long action plans geared at eradicating homelessness, the Bloomberg administration launched *Uniting for Solutions Beyond Shelter,* a ten-year plan to end chronic homelessness in New York City, in June of 2004.[9] The plan put forth ambitious goals regarding homeless prevention and shelter census reduction, with perhaps the most ambitious objective being the decline of homelessness by two-thirds in five years. The city's strategy to do this included a shift away from sheltering individuals and families in order to focus on prevention, discharge planning, rapid re-housing, and supportive housing.

The launching of the action plan and the PATH center processes marked the beginning of the city's new approach to dealing with family homelessness: census control. DHS responded to the conflicting realities of census reduction and a simultaneous increase in demand for shelter by implementing a tight "front door." In other words, DHS seemingly adopted a policy of intricate eligibility guidelines and application process to facilitate the rejection of those seeking shelter. At the same time, policy and efforts focused on bolstering permanent housing by imposing placement targets on providers and finding more efficient uses of housing subsidies. Unfortunately, DHS's housing programs would not succeed in producing the number of placements the city's homeless required.

In 2005, DHS launched the short-lived Housing Stability Plus (HSP) program. HSP offered a five-year housing subsidy to homeless families, chronically homeless single adults in shelter, and parents awaiting housing in order to reunite with children in foster care. The subsidy was set at market rates and decreased in value by 20% each year. This meant that a family receiving the HSP subsidy would have to make up that annual 20% reduction out-of-pocket. DHS presented HSP as an attempt to promote personal responsibility and self-sufficiency by encouraging work, and indeed the annual reduction in the subsidy necessitated that participants seek employment. Critics of the program felt, however, that the program's requirement of an active public assistance case discouraged participants from work: as a family's income increased as a result of gainful employment, its public assistance supplement decreased. This served to widen the gap between the family's income and its expenses, placing the family in danger of becoming homeless once again.[10] In addition, DHS was flooded with complaints on the quality and safety of HSP apartments. The program ultimately could not overcome these challenges and was discontinued by the end of 2007.

In the wake of the failed HSP, the city launched a new set of Housing Advantage Programs targeting specific populations, including children, families, and disabled heads of households. Beginning in the spring of 2007, the Work Advantage Program continued the housing policy of tying rental subsidies to employment initiatives.[11] Although it is too soon to evaluate the success of the new program, its design suggests that it, too, may fall the way of HSP. First, the term of the Work Advantage subsidy is quite short—one year with the option of renewal for a second year. Second, clients must save a required 10% to 20% of their employment income to receive the program's savings benefit, wherein the city will match any funds saved at the end of the program. Finally, although the program requires that participants work, it does nothing to guarantee employment sustainability so that families can continue paying rent once the subsidy expires after the second year. In fact, the Work Advantage subsidy is contingent upon the employability of homeless parents, many of whom face significant barriers to employment. Most of today's homeless parents tend to be young, single mothers with young children who have little to no work experience and lack a high school education. These parents are unlikely to find jobs that pay well enough to support their families and contribute to rental payments, let alone sustain themselves after the tenure of the subsidy ends.

The Current State of Family Homelessness

June 2009 marked the five-year anniversary of the city's action plan to end homelessness, *Uniting for Solutions Beyond Shelter,* and found the metropolis no closer to meeting any of the plan's goals. The plan had specified five key outcome measures relating to family homelessness. These included a decrease in applications for shelter, families in shelter, and length of time in shelter, in addition to an increase in families exiting shelter to permanent housing and low-cost supportive housing. When the city had first announced its action plan in 2004, the family shelter census had reached an unprecedented high, with 9,347 families in shelter. Although the shelter census decreased by 15% during the two first years of the plan, it increased again almost to pre-plan levels by the end of fiscal year 2009 (see Figure 18). Thus despite the city's best efforts to control the shelter census, there has been no lasting progress in reducing the number of families in shelter. The number of families in shelter has reached unprecedented levels, with more than 10,300 residing in city shelters in October 2009, including more than 16,100 children, and the problem is only worsening.

Figure 18
Average Daily Family Shelter Census (New York City, 2004 to 2009)
Source: DHS *Critical Activities Reports, 2004 to 2009*

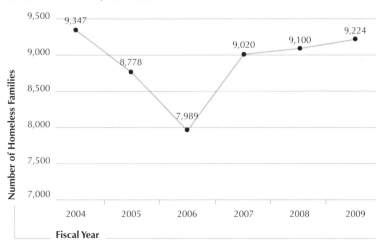

Figure 19

Number of Homeless Families Applying for Transitional Housing (New York City, 2002 to 2009)
Source: Department of Homeless Services, *Critical Activities Reports, 2002 to 2009*
Data includes multiple applications made by the same family.

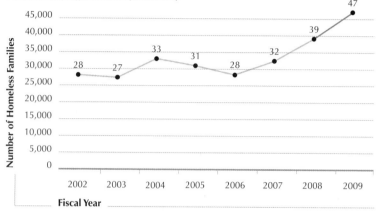

Finally, the city cannot achieve its permanent housing goals for homeless families because of the decreasing stock of affordable housing. The production of new affordable units continues to decline; during the 1960s, 360,000 low-income housing units were built, as opposed to only 83,000 during the 1990s.[14] Furthermore, the units of affordable housing under development target middle-income working families. In 2003, the Department of Housing and Urban Development pledged $50 million

Table 2
Family Placements and Length of Stay in Shelter
Source: Department of Homeless Services, *Critical Activities Report, 2003–2009*

Fiscal Year	Number of Families Placed in Permanent Housing	Families Placed in Permanent Housing as % of All Families Served	Average Length of Stay in Shelter in Days
2003	5,333	28%	303
2004	7,090	33%	341
2005	6,680	33%	344
2006	6,634	33%	344
2007	6,181	28%	325
2008	7,463	32%	350
2009	8,810	33%	292

for the creation of three hundred units of affordable housing in lower Manhattan. Eligibility rests with having an income between $50,000 and $85,000 a year and thus eliminates the segment of New York's population most in need of such housing.[15]

In 2003, Mayor Bloomberg announced his "New Housing Marketplace Plan," a ten-year plan to create and preserve 165,000 units of affordable housing. The plan included a Middle Class Housing Initiative that afforded roughly 32% of these units to moderate or middle-income families with the remaining 68% slated for households with income less than or equal to 80% of the Area Median Income ($39,700 for a single person or $56,700 for a family of four).[16] Homeless families in shelter, however, have incomes well below those considered low-income by the Mayor's initiative. Until the city has a reliable stock of low-income housing for homeless families, the burden will continue to fall on shelters to compensate for the shortage.

Shelters: Yesterday and Today

For years, many viewed New York City's shelters not as places of refuge for families but as destitute dwellings of last resort. In the early days, they were indeed stark, temporary, intimidating places. Families lived in gymnasiums, armories, and run-down hotels, and none were an appropriate place to call home. In contrast, most of today's Tier II family shelters are safe, clean, and private, with many offering family living suites, common areas, and on-site social services. Unfortunately, the process of obtaining a placement in this type of Tier II shelter has become a long and difficult one.

The Long Journey

A homeless family's journey into a New York City shelter begins at the PATH center. Once they complete their intake, most families are "conditionally" placed until DHS reaches a decision about their application; DHS has ten days to do so. DHS bases eligibility for families on a review of their previous two-year housing history to determine if the family has an alternative viable housing option to shelter. Families found eligible receive temporary housing; families found ineligible are discharged from shelter. If a family is found ineligible and reapplies within 90 days of their last determination, they are no longer guaranteed a conditional placement.[17] DHS finds families ineligible for a variety of reasons, including an incomplete housing history or the lack of a child's birth certificate.

Although an improvement on the grim EAU center, the PATH center was never intended to accommodate the high number of families that it must currently serve. This sometimes results in overcrowded waiting rooms and long lines that extend beyond the entrance door. While most eligible families are eventually placed in Tier II transitional housing facilities, the high census numbers force the city to continue the use of private hotels and cluster-site apartments. Most of these inferior units provide limited to no social or support services and are intended for temporary, conditional stays only.

Closing the Front Door to Shelter and the Rights of Families

As DHS seeks to reduce the family shelter census and meet the goals of the Mayor's action plan, homeless families pay the price as their right to shelter is undermined. Through the implementation of a complex and lengthy application process, DHS may be denying shelter to many families in need. Although the number of applications increased by 21% in fiscal year 2008, there was a 24% decrease in the eligibility rate, or 10% decrease in the number of eligible applications. Given the economic landscape, it is unlikely that the drop in eligible families was due to a decrease in need for shelter, but rather the result of the city's homeless policy. These numbers suggest that DHS tightened the front door in order to control its homeless family census. From fiscal year 2008 to fiscal year 2009, there was a 33% increase in the number of eligible applications, yet the eligibility rate stayed relatively flat (from 29% to 30%). The rise in eligible families during 2009 is likely due to DHS increasing bed capacity to meet a surge in applications for shelter driven by the recession. It remains to be seen whether DHS will continue to respond to rising demand by increasing bed capacity or if it will opt for a tighter front door policy, as it appears to have done in the past. Moreover, there is evidence to suggest that the city's efforts did not translate into housing stability for many families.

Since the first year of the Mayor's action plan, the proportion of eligible applications that corresponds to repeat families (families who have been in shelters in the past and returned) increased from 26% to almost 40%.[18]

At the same time, the urgency placed on the rapid re-housing of homeless families has come at the expense of placement stability. By rushing shelter providers to quickly place families into permanent housing, providers must compromise the quality of the placement and in some cases move out families who are not ready to exit the shelter system. Consequently, the percentage of families that leave shelter and return (recidivism rate) within one year has increased by 50%, from 2% in the 2004 fiscal year (pre-plan) to 3% in fiscal year 2008, while the two-year rate has increased by 57%, from 7% in fiscal year 2004 to 10% in fiscal year 2009. Another indicator that the city's policy is resulting in a "revolving front door" is the increase in the number of repeat eligible families — not newcomers to the system—as a proportion of all families found eligible for shelter (see Figure 20).

Figure 20
Percentage of Repeat Families Among Eligible (New York City, 2002 to 2008)
Source: Department of Homeless Services, *Critical Activities Report, 2002 to 2008*

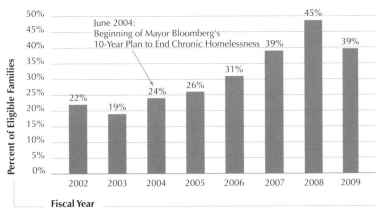

Something New Is Something Old
In its search for makeshift solutions to the modern homeless crisis, the city has recycled some old ideas. At the beginning of the millennium, officials weighed various options to reduce the almost $1 billion shelter

burden.[19] Proposals that were received with fanfare in the 1980s and 1990s and later abandoned, such as housing families in mobile homes or congregate shelters, and putting EAU services in each borough, were once again under discussion.

Among the explored solutions, the city talked about evicting families from shelters if they rejected worthy apartments, and even discussed desperate measures such as housing families in retired cruise ships, docked at public piers. Putting indigent or mentally or physically ill individuals out to sea on islands or floating facilities has a long history in New York City. Fortunately, the idea was abandoned once officials realized the cost of refitting the ships would be too expensive.[20] Had it come into reality, turning cruise ships into housing could have led to more squalor and isolation for homeless families than the Midtown welfare hotels ever did.

Even welfare hotels, which in the 1980s accounted for the majority of placements and later became near extinct, were once again running at peak capacity. Other temporary placements, such as scattered-site housing, were also on the rise. In 2000, the Department of Homeless Services began renting out apartments from private landlords in order to house homeless families pushed out of crowded Tier II shelters, and placed the provision of services to these families into the hands of those private landlords. The use of this scattered-site housing, one of the most expensive and least effective forms of temporary shelter, grew tremendously. In January 2001, just sixty-one families lived in scattered-site units, the *New York Times* reported.[21] A year later, in February 2002, that number had risen to 1,224 at a monthly cost of $3.7 million, or $44 million a year. Today, almost 1,400 families are housed in scatter-site units, now renamed "cluster sites" and over 2,300 families continue to reside in hotels.[22]

As most of these old ideas came under media and public scrutiny, the city had to confront the economic challenge of housing more homeless families than ever before. By 2004, homeless policy was at the forefront of the Bloomberg agenda. Given the failure of previous policies and the rising cost of shelter, the administration's focus shifted from sheltering individuals and families to rapid re-housing strategies. However, by 2008, this policy nagged at the administration's coattails.

We are now at the midpoint of Mayor Bloomberg's action plan to end chronic homelessness, *Uniting for Solutions Beyond Shelter*, and it is clear that the city fell far short of its five-year goal of reducing homelessness by two-thirds. In fact, there has been little progress, if any, in any success outcome measures laid out by the Mayor's action plan: the number of families applying for shelter is higher, housing placements as a percentage of all families in shelter are down, and recidivism is up. In September 2008, the city settled a 25-year long lawsuit, *McCain* v. *Koch*, guaranteeing the right to shelter for homeless families, in addition to a myriad of provisions to assist applicant families in procuring relevant documents and ensuring placement into safe housing. However, although it is too soon to evaluate the effect of this settlement on homeless policy in New York City, DHS continues to implement policies and procedures that effectively turn away homeless families and close the front door to shelter. The city's ambitious ten-year action plan to end homelessness brought a tighter front door to shelter and a focus on permanent placements. Ironically, it is this very approach that shatters the administration's hope of ending family homelessness and causes the system to continually grow beyond its control.

Notes

[1] Linda Gibbs, City Council Testimony, New York City Council Meeting, City Hall, New York, 18 September 2002.

[2] Ibid.

[3] Ibid.

[4] Michael Cooper, "Jail Reopens as a Shelter for Families," *New York Times,* 12 August 2002.

[5] Jennifer Steinhauer, "A Jail Becomes a Shelter, and Maybe a Mayor's Albatross," *New York Times,* 13 August 2002.

[6] Nina Bernstein, "Mentally Ill Boy Kills Himself in Shelter Hotel," *New York Times,* 8 August 2002.

[7] New York City Family Homelessness Special Master Panel, *Report on the Emergency Assistance Unit and Shelter Eligibility Determination,* June 2004.

[8] See Press Release "Mayor Bloomberg Opens Temporary Intake Office for Families Seeking Shelter and Announces $30 million Commitment to Create

New Permanent Center," November 16, 2004, http://home.nyc.gov/html/dhs/html/press/pr111604.shtml

[9] In June 2004, Mayor Bloomberg released *Uniting for Solutions Beyond Shelter,* a ten-year plan to end chronic homelessness in New York City. The plan is available at: www.nyc.gov/html/endinghomelessness/html/action-plan/action_plan.shtml

[10] Institute for Children and Poverty, *The Instabilities of Housing Stability Plus* (New York: Institute for Children and Poverty, 2006).

[11] The Work Advantage Program was launched in 2007 as a one-year (with option to renew for a second term) rental subsidy at market rates. The program is available to families and individuals working at least 20 hours a week and has no public assistance requirements. Participants are required to pay $50 directly to landlords and to save 10% to 20% of their income, which the city will match at the end of the term.

[12] Institute for Children and Poverty, *Failure at the Four Year Mark* (New York: Institute for Children and Poverty, 2008).

[13] Figures based on New York City's fiscal year, which runs from July to June.

[14] Steinhauer, "A Jail Becomes A Shelter and Maybe a Mayor's Albatross," *New York Times,* 13 August 2002."

[15] United States Department of Housing and Urban Development, *Martinez, Pataki and Bloomberg Announce $50 Million Affordable Housing Initiative in Lower Manhattan* (New York: HUD, 2003). Available at: http://www.hud.gov/news.

[16] New York City Independent Budget Office, *Fiscal Brief: The Mayor's New Housing Marketplace Plan: Progress to Date and Prospect for Completion* (New York: Independent Budget Office, 2007).

[17] As of March 2006, families who reapply within 90 days of having been found ineligible for shelter will not receive placement unless they meet certain exceptions. These exceptions are: material change since last application (new information or documents), immediate danger or medical needs, actual eviction, and domestic violence or child abuse.

[18] New York City Department of Homeless Services, *Critical Activities Report, Family Services; Fiscal years 2005 and 2009.* New York: New York City Department of Homeless Services.

[19] Linda Gibbs, City Council Testimony.

[20] Leslie Kaufman, "Manhattan: No Cruise Ships for Homeless," *New York Times,* 18 June 2003.

[21] Nina Bernstein, "Many More Children Calling New York City Shelters Home," *New York Times,* 13 February 2002; New York City Department of Homeless Services, Office of Policy and Planning, *Critical Activities Report, Family Services: Fiscal Year 2003* (New York: Department of Homeless Services, 2003), 2.

[22] New York City Department of Homeless Services, *Critical Activities Report, Family Services: Fiscal Year 2009* (New York: New York City Department of Homeless Services, 2009).

Homeless Children at New York City Family Shelters

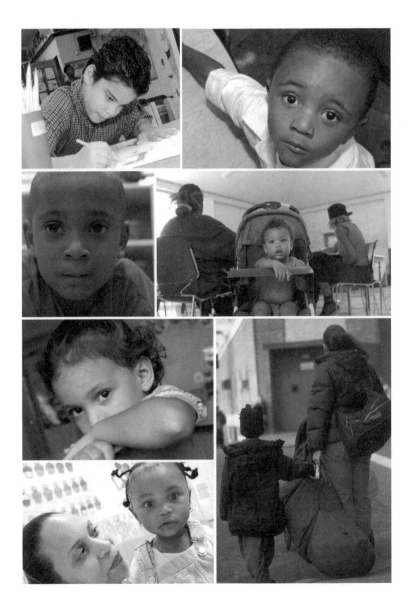

**Emergency Assistance Unit
Bronx, New York**

Tier I Congregate Emergency Shelters

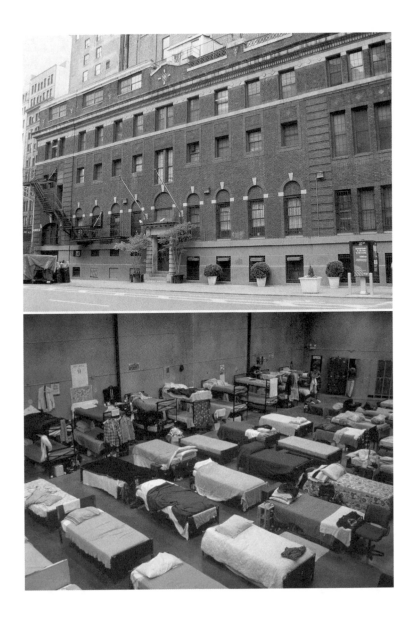

Welfare Hotel and Motel

Martinique Hotel

Scattered-Site Housing

Tier II Transitional Housing, New Communities

On-Site After-school Programs

Family Literacy and Employment Training

Crisis Nurseries

Health Services and GED Alternative Schooling

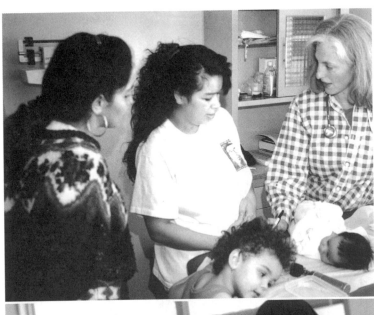

Saratoga Family Inn
Queens, New York

6 Coming Home
The Reality of Housing Policy

As the homeless crisis worsens, the city continues to focus on providing immediate emergency housing to families until they are able to leave the system. But what happens when they are ready to find a home of their own? The reality is that there is little affordable housing available. Efforts to achieve what seems like a relatively simple goal—renovating or building more affordable units—have exploded into a highly charged debate.

In the policy and homeless advocates' agendas, the argument centers on whether efforts should go to building permanent or transitional housing. Those who argue for more permanent housing believe that a massive investment in new, affordable apartments is the only way to help families escape from poverty. While agreeing with the need for more affordable units, advocates for transitional shelter argue that a single-minded focus on building new housing addresses neither the depth of social service needs faced by homeless families, nor the complexity of the current housing situation and housing policy.

Recent homeless policy has embraced a Housing First or rapid re-housing approach, presenting it as the sole cost-effective solution to homelessness. Responding to limited capacity and increasing use and cost of shelter, Housing First strategies focus on limited shelter use and rapid movement to permanent housing. Across the nation over two hundred and twenty communities have committed to action plans to end homelessness, mostly designed around Housing First and rapid re-housing strategies.[1] However, the real problem is that communities still have to face the current housing affordability crisis and a contradictory federal housing agenda that has considerably cut funding for low-income housing programs.

Losing The Battle: The Declining Housing Stock

While the need for affordable housing continues to grow, the nation's supply of units has been on a thirty-year downward spiral. The stock of such housing has declined so significantly that, by 1995, the gap between low-income rental households and low-cost rental units had widened to over 4.4 million.[2] In 1999, a landmark federal study revealed that, from 1996 to 1998, the number of affordable units fell by 19%, or 1.3 million units. This drop was largely due to the demolition of distressed properties and a shift of privately-owned subsidized units to open rental market rates.[3] Housing affordability continues to be a challenge in the 2000s, with the number of households that spend more than half their income on rent increasing by 30%, from 13.8 million to 17.9 million, between 2001 and 2007. Moreover, in 2007, nearly three-quarters of these households were in the bottom quarter of the income distribution.[4]

Historically, low-income housing has been the domain of the federal government but beginning with the Reagan administration, government essentially abandoned the subsidized housing business and the city has been unable to pick up the slack. Specifically, the Department of Housing and Development's (HUD) funding for low-income housing decreased by 48% from the beginning of the 1980s to 2004 (see Figure 21).[5] In fact, from 2004 to 2008, funding for low-income housing assistance fell more than two billion dollars.[6] At the city level, from 2001 to 2008 the New York City Housing Authority (NYCHA) has lost more than $600 million in federal money provided through HUD. NYCHA's current budget deficit has already resulted in cuts in community-based programs offered by the agency, and forced the conversion of its 21 projects into Section 8 housing.[7] New York has also lost thousands of Section 8 vouchers: 11,841 between 2004 and 2006.[8]

New York City: Unique Challenges

The challenge of keeping people affordably housed and out of homeless shelters is acutely felt in New York, a city where land is scarce and the real estate market is tight. Here, the cost of rent is the highest in the country, with the market rate for a one-bedroom apartment in Manhattan

Figure 21

HUD Spending on Low-income Housing (Billions of Constant 2004 Dollars)
Source: National Low Income Housing Coalition, 2004

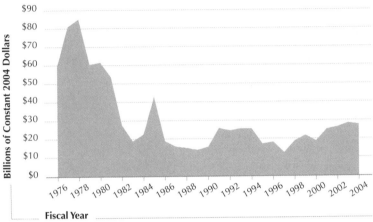

currently standing at $2,200 a month, and $950, $900, and $706 per month for Queens, Brooklyn, and the Bronx, respectively (see Table 3).[9] Between 2002 and 2005 alone, rents in the city increased 17%.[10] Unlike the citizens of other large American cities, more New Yorkers rent than own, with almost 600,000 residents spending more than half their income on rent.[11] In a market where a 4% vacancy rate is considered normal turnover, the 2008 vacancy rate for low-income rental units (those renting for $500 or less) was so small that it was not reported. Units renting between $500 and $799 had a mere 1.5% vacancy rate in 2008.[12]

Meanwhile, the income gap between the city's richest and poorest residents continues to grow. By the mid-2000s, New York had the widest

Table 3 New York City Housing Costs Source: New York City Rent Guidelines Board	
Borough	Average Market Rental Rate for a One-Bedroom Apartment
Manhattan	$2,200/month
Queens	$950/month
Brooklyn	$900/month
Bronx	$706/month

income gap in the country, with high incomes 8.7 times greater than low incomes. Between the late 1980s and the early 2000s, the average income of the bottom 20% of New York City households increased by only $882, or 5.4%. Wealthier households in the top fifth fared far better, with their average income rising by $38,681, or 35%, a rate of increase six times faster than that of the bottom fifth. By the mid-2000s, the average income of New York City's richest households was almost fifteen and a half times that of the city's poorest.[13]

In keeping with these trends, between 2002 and 2008, the number of low-rent units decreased while the number of high rent units increased. In 2008, the number of vacant units renting for less than $500 dropped so low that the New York City Department of Housing Preservation and Development could not include information about such housing in its most recent survey, while units with rents between $500 and $999 decreased by 45%. On the other hand, available units with rents between $1,000 and $2,499 increased by 70% (see Figure 22).[14] These figures reflect neighborhood gentrification, with formerly low-rent enclaves from Williamsburg, Brooklyn, to Harlem and the East Village, to the Lower East Side of Manhattan becoming the focus of high-rent construction and renovation.

Figure 22
Percent Change in Available Units by Rent Amount, New York City (2002–2008)
Source: *New York City Housing and Vacancy Survey, 2002 and 2008*

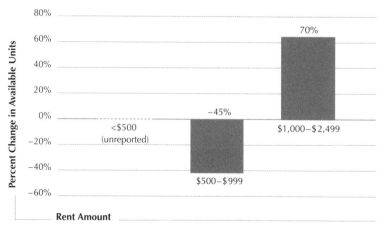

Gentrification across the city has placed low-income residents in peril, as those living on the fringe of the rental market can no longer afford the rent in the areas where they have always lived. Thousands of New Yorkers have been priced out of their own neighborhoods, making room for the influx of middle-class newcomers willing to pay higher rents. In recent years, increasing attention has been paid to the effects of gentrification on the precariously housed and homeless. Displaced low-income families must piece together temporary living situations, doubling and tripling up with friends and relatives, before eventually turning to the city's emergency shelter system. Newly gentrifying neighborhoods in Manhattan, Brooklyn, and Queens have been associated with spikes in shelter applications and increased incidences of family homelessness.[15]

Possible Solutions: Proposals from Advocates

What are possible solutions to the city's deep-rooted housing problems? Housing advocates consistently call for increased rental subsidies, as well as for the creation of more housing linked with supportive services. Although both initiatives would be a step in the right direction, neither offers an all-encompassing solution, particularly in light of the scope of the issues and current financial and political realities.

Rental Subsidies

There is no question that families on the brink of homelessness would benefit from an increase in rental subsidies. In 2005, the state launched the Family Eviction Prevention Supplement (FEPS) program, increasing subsidies for families on welfare from $286 to up to $850 per month for a family of three; however, this amount is barely the rental market rate for a one-bedroom apartment in New York City, and totally insufficient to afford an apartment for a family of three.[16] In addition to limited state rental subsidies, families are also experiencing the effects of federal cuts in the rental voucher program. Current Section 8 listings are filled; poor families on the list endure multi-year waits for a voucher, only to discover that there is a severe shortage of private landlords participating in the program. Likewise, many families desperately search for Section 8-eligible housing, only to have their voucher expire before they find it. In 2001 alone, when the program was at its zenith, 1,000 Section 8 rental vouchers committed to homelessness went unused.[17]

Even if rent subsidies were to increase, ensuring that homeless families could successfully navigate the rental market would be difficult at best. In order to access adequate housing, families face an array of obstacles including landlord discrimination, poor credit, employment instability, and public assistance sanctions. In addition, when the market remains extremely competitive, landlords and brokers know they can expect rents well above market rate as well as hefty fees and security deposits far exceeding those offered by current subsidies.

Supportive Housing

Another initiative backed by housing advocates is more permanent supportive housing with attached social services. Many transitional Tier II shelters already use an approach similar to this model, providing families with extensive support services to prevent future bouts of homelessness. The supportive housing approach is different in that it requires a significant amount of up-front capital. Additionally, the level and amount of necessary services may be too extensive to be provided efficiently and successfully in an unstructured, permanent residential environment.

The up-front costs are perhaps the biggest drawbacks to supportive housing, which necessitates the creation of housing units where individuals and families could be placed. In 2005, the New York/New York III Supportive Housing Agreement was made between the state and the city, pledging to build 9,000 supportive housing units in New York City over 10 years. Capital costs for NY/NY III are estimated at $1 billion, in addition to approximately $156 million per year in operating costs, over the 10-year timeframe. Unfortunately, 9,000 units would not even be sufficient to house the city's current number of homeless families, let alone individuals. In fact, of the 9,000 new units, only 1,150 are targeted for homeless families.[18]

Another concern is that there is very little consensus among various stakeholders on what the idea of supportive housing means in practice. Though it has become a trendy initiative, supportive housing does not appear to be well thought out, as a vast range of housing-plus-services models fall under the umbrella of "supportive housing": some proponents advocate for permanent housing with off-site, community-based social services, others call for more temporary units with on-site services. Whether services are on- or off-site, and whether the apartments are permanent or temporary, makes an enormous difference in both the costs of supportive housing and its effectiveness. This is particularly important given the tendency for permanent housing models to equate off-site services with referrals and linkages to existing social service system programs. Frequently, such programs have already failed to meet the needs of families and keep them out of shelter.

Before New York can undertake such a project, advocates must come to a consensus on what exactly supportive housing would look like. Would families in need of services be mandated to seek them? Would there be penalties, or even evictions, if they refused? The state must also determine how much supervision and investment supportive housing would entail. Even with these critical elements addressed, the question would remain—how could the city assume the costs of creating the necessary units of affordable housing and the additional costs of providing expensive social services?

Nonetheless, advocates of supportive housing argue that although the approach would require millions of dollars of up-front capital, the city would ultimately save money since homelessness itself is so expensive. Arguing that homeless people with problems use the highest-cost public systems, advocates claim that the alternatives are more expensive than the creation and maintenance of supportive units. Problematically, they frequently list the alternatives as jail cells, mental hospitals, or emergency room beds, services that are certainly more expensive, but by no means the only alternative. Moreover, these are systems used heavily by single adults living on the street, not families. In fact, the current assessment on the cost of homelessness is based on the single homeless adult population and its service utilization patterns. It does not represent the needs of families, nor the real cost of family homelessness for families and communities.

At a time of major fiscal constraint, the city is hardly in a position to indulge in an initiative with such large up-front costs. It is simply not financially feasible, especially in light of the fact that a massive transitional housing system already exists in New York City. This system could fairly easily be transformed to provide all the necessary services described in a supportive housing model, but without the massive initial costs.

A New Dialogue: From Housing to Shelters

Any real and meaningful plan to end family homelessness must start with political honesty. As we have seen, the government has not, and in all likelihood cannot, produce low-income housing on any sufficient scale in the near future. Every night, thousands of New York City families with children call a shelter their home. From there, they commute to work and school, celebrate birthdays and holidays, and experience the joys and sorrows of childhood and parenthood. These families cannot afford to wait yet another decade or more until politics and finances possibly align to allow for the construction of more low-income housing units. We must come to grips with reality: for the immediate and foreseeable future, we will have to work within the context of what currently exists. In order to do so, we need to better understand today's homeless families and their immediate and long-term needs.

Issues like domestic violence, unemployment, and a lack of education weigh heavily here and may in fact be the main reasons for New Yorkers' homelessness. The first step towards a solution must involve a careful look at the root causes of family homelessness and, naturally, the characteristics of homeless parents and children themselves.

Notes

[1] National Alliance to End Homelessness, *Promising Strategies to End Family Homelessness* (Washington, D.C.: NAEH, June 2006), 1.

[2] Jennifer Daskal, *In Search of Shelter: The Growing Shortage of Affordable Housing Units* (Washington, D.C.: Center on Budget and Policy Priorities, 1998).

[3] U.S. Department of Housing and Urban Development, *Waiting In Vain: An Update on America's Housing Crisis* (Washington, D.C.: U.S. Department of Housing and Urban Development, 1999).

[4] Joint Center For Housing Studies of Harvard University, *The State of The Nation's Housing, 2009*. (Cambridge, MA: Joint Center For Housing Studies of Harvard University. 2008), 40.

[5] Cushing Dolbeare, Irene Baslow Saraf, and Sheila Crowley, *Changing Priorities: The Federal Budget and Housing Assistance 1976–2005*. (The National Low Income Housing Coalition, October 2004), A-8.

[6] Douglass Rice and Barbara Sard, *Decade of Neglect Has Weakened Federal Low-Income Housing Programs*. (Washington, D.C.: Center on Budget and Policy Priorities, February 24, 2009).

[7] Manny Fernandez, "Housing Cuts Are Proposed to Close Budget Gap," *New York Times*, 30 May 2008.

[8] Center on Budget and Policy Priorities, *Housing Vouchers Funded in New York Under Pending Proposals* (Washington, D.C.: CBPP, November 1, 2006).

[9] NYC Rental Guidelines Board, *Housing Cost: Where Can You Find the Lowest Rents?*, http://www.housingnyc.com/html/guide/location.html

[10] New York City Department of Housing Preservation and Development, *2005 Housing and Vacancy Survey: Initial Findings*. (New York: New York City Department of Housing, Preservation, and Development, 2005) 5.

[11] Ibid., 9.

[12] New York City Department of Housing Preservation and Development, *Selected Initial Findings of the 2008 New York City Housing and Vacancy Survey*, 4.

[13] Trudi Renwick, *Pulling Apart in New York: An Analysis of Income Trends in New York State* (New York: Fiscal Policy Institute, 2008).

[14] New York City Department of Housing Preservation and Development, *Selected Initial Findings of the 2008 New York City Housing and Vacancy Survey*, 4; New York City Department of Housing Preservation and Development, *2002 New York City Housing and Vacancy Survey*.

[15] Institute for Children and Poverty, *The Cost of Good Intentions: Gentrification and Homelessness in Upper Manhattan* (New York: Institute for Children and Poverty, 2006); Institute for Children and Poverty, *Pushed Out: The Hidden Costs of Gentrification: Displacement and Homelessness* (New York: Institute for Children and Poverty, 2009).

[16] The Family Eviction Prevention Supplement Program, FEPS, was launched in May 2005. FEPS is a state program that pays back rent and higher ongoing rent for some families in need of assistance who currently receive public assistance. Prior to FEPS, the state assisted families with rent payments through Jiggetts relief.

[17] Linda Gibbs, City Council Testimony, New York City Council Meeting, City Hall, New York, 18 September 2002.

[18] Supportive Housing Network of New York, "Funding the Solution to Homelessness: An Analysis of the New York/New York III Agreement," www.shnny.org

7 | A Poverty of Adults
Homeless Parents Today

Twenty-five years ago, the typical homeless parent in New York City was a thirty-five-year-old mother with a high school education and two adolescent children. She had probably worked at some point before becoming dependent on public assistance, and she was more likely to have been married to the father of her children than homeless mothers today. An overcrowded living situation, a personal crisis, an eviction, or a lack of housing options brought her to the EAU for temporary shelter placement in a welfare hotel, and eventually, permanent housing.

Things have changed considerably in the intervening years, however. Today's homeless parent is most likely a twenty-six-year-old mother of one or two children. Without a high school diploma, she has only worked for brief stints at minimum wage, and she now finds herself unemployed and on public assistance as the welfare time clock is running out (see Table 4). In many cases, her homeless journey began after fleeing a violent partner.[1] No longer does her arrival at the PATH center (the city's family intake center since 2004) signify the beginning of a journey from shelter to affordable housing, but rather the start of a protracted battle just to be recognized as "eligible" for shelter under current New York City regulations.

Today, a new generation of homeless parents has replaced the welfare hotel dwellers of the 1980s. They are significantly younger, more likely to be victims of domestic violence, and often foster care survivors. In New York City, 57% of these homeless parents are Black and 38% are Hispanic (see Figure 23). Eighty-eight percent of them are single mothers, with limited social support systems.[2] Twenty years ago, being homeless

Table 4
Homeless Parent Profile: New York City (1987 and 2002)
Source: Institute for Children and Poverty Data (n=408)

	1987	2002
Sex (female)	92%	99%
Age (< 25 years)	27%	42%
Marital status (single)	60%	98%
Education (< High School)	38%	55%
Foster/Limbo Care as a child	5%	30%
Employment		
Employed > 6 months	60%	10%
Employed > 1 year	36%	5%

was seen as a last resort for those living on the brink of poverty. Many homeless parents today have found that instability and dependence are a way of life, so that coming to a shelter has been almost like coming home. Of the younger homeless mothers (18 to 21 years), roughly 21% spent part of their childhood in a shelter, and 20% were in foster care as children.[3] Thirty-four percent of these young women grew up in a family

Figure 23
Racial Profile of New York City Families: All Families vs. Homeless Families
Source: U.S. Census Bureau; NYC Department of Homeless Services, *Critical Activities Report, 2009*

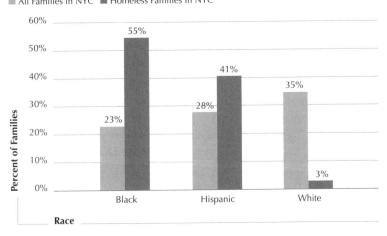

receiving public assistance, while the rest were children of the working poor.[4] There is even evidence to suggest that today's homeless crisis is a direct outgrowth of the mid-1980s homeless crisis. New York City homeless parents who are twenty-one years old or younger are almost twice as likely as those over twenty-one to have been homeless as a child.[5] But regardless of their previous experiences with the shelter system, today's homeless parents face a unique set of obstacles that must be identified in order to properly address them.

Domestic Violence

Victims of domestic violence often live in transience and chaos: fleeing an abuser, doubling up with friends and relatives, staying at a domestic violence shelter, and often returning to the abuser once again. In fact, the average victim returns to her abuser six times before making a final break towards independence.[6] For poorer victims, this process is an even greater struggle, since many of these women lack the family support, financial assets, and community resources necessary for escaping violence. When their options run out, many find themselves homeless.

Figure 24
Homeless Parents Who Experienced Domestic Violence and Who Entered Shelters As a Result
Source: Institute for Children and Poverty Data; *n=471*

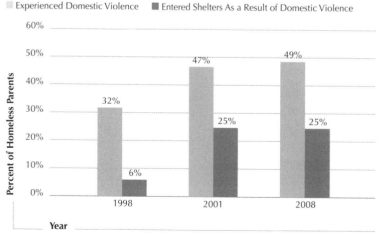

Domestic violence victims are one of the fastest growing groups of shelter seekers. Forty-nine percent of all homeless parents have a history of domestic violence, and one in four cite such abuse as their primary reason for seeking shelter (see Figure 24).[7] This legacy of violence is often passed on to the children of the victims. Thirty-one percent of homeless children have witnessed domestic violence, and observing such behavior in the home is a strong predictor of future victimization and abuse.[8] In fact, research shows that boys who witness violence by their fathers are twice as likely to abuse their partners as adults than boys who were not exposed to domestic violence.[9]

In response to this growing crisis, New York City launched a major media campaign in 2001 to promote a public hotline that victims fleeing violence could call. The hotline was so successful that calls have risen 60% since 1997. However, from 2001 to 2008, bed capacity in domestic violence shelters expanded by an average of only 6% annually, causing the overflow of domestic violence victims into the emergency housing family intake center and into the "mainstream" family shelter system.[10] In 2008, police responded to 234,988 domestic violence incidents, yet there are only 2,144 domestic violence emergency shelter beds citywide.[11] Currently, homeless families requesting shelter who give any indications of or claim domestic violence are referred to the No Violence Again office (NOVA). If found eligible for the NOVA program, these families are placed in a domestic violence shelter or, in the case of a lack of capacity, are referred back to DHS and placed immediately in a homeless shelter.

Nonetheless, the city's shelter system remains ill equipped to care for the unique needs of these individuals. In particular, the system's hotels and cluster-site housing (temporary lodging in isolated apartment units), is the least suitable option for victims of domestic violence. This form of housing neglects the safety and emotional needs of a family by giving the apartment's landlord, rather than the city or a social service agency, the all-important task of providing social services. In most instances, the family's critical needs go unmet. In addition, there are serious security concerns for families with histories of domestic violence. Unlike Tier IIs and domestic violence shelters, cluster sites have only limited security.

Foster and Limbo Care

Many homeless parents also have a connection to the city's foster and limbo care system, some moving directly from these to homelessness. ("Limbo care" is a placement in kinship or informal care with friends or relatives.) Approximately 30% of all homeless parents have spent part of their childhood in foster or limbo care; this percentage is higher for young mothers (under 22 years old).[12]

Homeless parents with a history of foster or limbo care often have faced a different, more daunting set of obstacles. Forty-seven percent experienced abuse or neglect as children, as opposed to only 14% of their non-foster care counterparts. These parents are also more than twice as likely to have experienced or seen domestic violence as children than homeless parents who were not in such care. More than half had their first child when they were in their teens and are more likely to have been homeless before (See Table 5).[13]

Table 5 Comparison of Homeless Parents: with and without a Foster or Limbo Care History Source: Institute for Children and Poverty; *n=471*		
Homeless Parents	Foster or Limbo Care History	No Foster or Limbo Care History
Experienced abuse or neglect as a child	47%	14%
Experienced or witnessed domestic violence as a child	63%	28%
Homeless more than once	55%	31%
Had their first child in their teens	51%	44%

In contrast to the increase in homeless mothers with foster and limbo care histories, there has been a decrease in their own children's experiences with the foster care system. The number of homeless parents with a foster and limbo care history who currently have an open child welfare case has dropped considerably, from 73% in 1993 to only 17% in 2008. Additionally, fewer of these parents have lost their own children to foster care, with most current involvements being preventive services or open investigations. In fact, the foster care population has dropped nearly 40% from 28,215 in 2002, to 16,947 in 2008.[14]

Domestic violence is among the top reasons for family homelessness, with one-quarter of homeless women citing it as the direct cause of their homelessness.[15] This, coupled with the simultaneous decrease in homeless parents with open child welfare cases, may suggest that the possibility of losing a child to foster care could be the impetus for a family to enter a homeless shelter. So many of these parents experienced foster or limbo care themselves that they may be more likely to leave a dangerous situation and prevent their own children from entering the system. For these families the shelter system plays the role of a form of family foster care, where, rather than surrendering a child, a mother keeps her family together in a safer environment.

Teen Pregnancy

While teenage pregnancy is on the decline nationwide, it is on the rise within the city's homeless population. Forty-seven percent of all homeless heads of households had their first child while a teenager (see Figure 25).[16] Furthermore, the number of young mothers entering shelter has increased considerably. These parents face many obstacles in life, including an incomplete education, dependence on public assistance, and a history

Figure 25
Age When Homeless Women Became Pregnant with Their First Child
Source: Institute for Children and Poverty Data; *n=323*

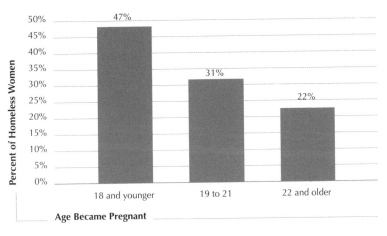

of abuse. Coupled with homelessness, the challenges for these teen mothers become nearly insurmountable.

A 2003 study noted that over three-quarters of these young parents first had intercourse before age seventeen, and one-third by age fifteen (see Figure 26). In 65% of these cases, a baby was born within one year of the onset of sexual activity.[17] Most of these women continue a cycle of family poverty and teenage pregnancy, as 53% are themselves the products of adolescent childbearing.

Figure 26
Age at Which Homeless Teen Mothers First Had Sex, New York City
Source: Institute for Children and Poverty; "Children Having Children," 2003.

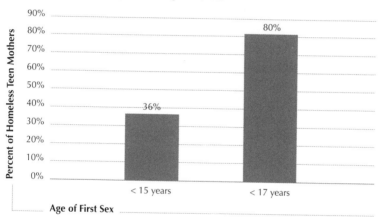

These teenage mothers also demonstrate a profound lack of knowledge about birth control. One in two did not believe birth control was important, 37% did not know how to obtain it, and 42% did not know how to use it (see Figure 27). Equally disturbing, 41% did not even know they were pregnant until the second trimester, missing a critical opportunity for prenatal care.[18]

To make things worse, these mothers face limited resources and failing safety nets caused by diminishing support systems. Many of them have already experienced poverty and homelessness: 32% were homeless before the age of eighteen, and 42% have been homeless more than once.[19] With

Figure 27
Birth Control Knowledge among Homeless Teenage Mothers, New York City
Source: Institute for Children and Poverty Data; *n=323*

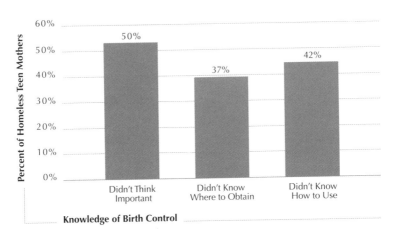

the added burden of early motherhood, it is difficult for these young women to obtain a higher education, which can lead to greater financial instability.

Job Readiness

In addition to facing domestic violence, foster care, and teen pregnancy issues, homeless mothers also have to find ways to support their families financially. These parents tend to fall into two categories: the unemployed, a large percentage of whom have never held a job, and the under-employed, who piece together part-time employment with substandard pay.

Unemployed homeless parents face multiple barriers to finding work. Almost one-fifth (18%) have never held a job and lack basic knowledge of work protocol and etiquette.[20] The majority read at a sixth grade level, have never used a computer, and do not possess the reading, writing, and math skills required for many positions. Some have criminal records or substance abuse problems that make them less likely to be hired. The inherent difficulties of a life in poverty (including medical problems, transportation issues, and a lack of childcare), coupled with the social stigma of being homeless, reduces the appeal of homeless parents to potential employers.

Under-employed homeless parents, in contrast, have already over-come the initial challenge of finding work. However, they often hold part-time, short-term positions in the service sector and have not acquired the skills necessary to advance to positions with higher salaries, increased responsibilities, and job security. It is estimated that 31% of homeless parents work; the majority earn minimum wage without benefits in places such as fast food outlets and retail stores.[21] Without a living wage and benefits, these parents are part of a growing group of working poor: working parents who, in increasing numbers, are unable to maintain a permanent home.

Compared to low-income heads of household who are not home-less, homeless heads of household are less likely to be employed and have had more disadvantages. While the share of low-income parents that are employed has increased, approximately three-quarters of homeless parents are unemployed. Homeless parents also have a more erratic work history and limited education. Seventy-four percent of low-income housed parents graduated from high school, as opposed to only 55% of homeless parents.[22]

Clearly, homeless parents lack basic education and skills to a far greater extent than their housed counterparts. This deficit makes it even more difficult for them to find and maintain employment that will pay enough to allow them to escape homelessness and stabilize their families.

Table 6

Qualifications Needed for Public Assistance Recipients to Participate in a Job Training Program vs. the Typical Homeless Female Head of Household
Source: Institute for Children and Poverty Data

The Typical Job Training Program Requires that the Candidate	The Typical Homeless Female Head of Household
Be job ready	Has little work experience
Have a High School diploma	Has a tenth grade education
Read at 8th grade level or higher	Reads at the 6th grade level
Possess basic computer skills, such as typing	Has few employable job skills
Provide their own day care	Has limited access to day care
Have no substance abuse history	Often has a substance abuse history
Provide their own transportation	Cannot afford transportation cost
Have a permanent address	Does not have a permanent address

Furthermore, homeless parents are frequently ineligible for traditional job training programs, which require a minimum level of education and skills, often higher than they tend to have, putting them at an even further disadvantage (see Table 6).

Welfare Reform

Ensuring that homeless parents have employable skills has become more crucial since the welfare reforms of 1996. The Personal Responsibility and Work Opportunity Reconciliation Act was designed to put "work first" and eliminate life-long welfare dependence. Families can only receive federal Family Assistance (FA) benefits for a total of five years in their lifetime and they are required to be working or in job training within two years of receiving aid.

In keeping with this new emphasis on work, New York City's welfare offices have been transformed into job centers, and eligible, unemployed adults are required to participate in the Work Experience Program (WEP), the country's largest public jobs program. WEP places participants in internships within city agencies, where workers receive below-minimum wage rates for jobs that once paid a union salary. In addition to the issues of a living wage, "work-first" programs do not address the most basic needs of unemployed and under-employed homeless families: housing, education, and social support services. In practice, these programs actually run counter to the intentions of the welfare reform law, which is to lift families out of poverty and give them economic independence.

The shift from welfare to workfare has had one intended effect: reducing the welfare rolls. The number of New Yorkers receiving public assistance declined dramatically, from more than 1.4 million in 1995 to approximately 336,000 by 2008 (see Figure 28).[23] Where do these families go when they leave the welfare rolls? When the economy was growing in the late 1990s, former welfare recipients were more easily able to find full-time jobs, even if barely at minimum wage.[24] In fact, from 1996 to 2002, the poverty rate for single mothers fell from 42% to 34%. However, by 2001, the economy weakened and such employment became more and more difficult to find. It is estimated that 40% of those single mothers

Figure 28
Decline in Public Assistance Recipients (New York City, 1995 to 2008)
Source: Human Resources Administration

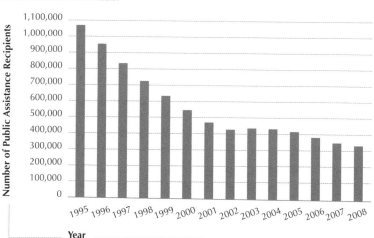

who had left the welfare rolls returned.[25] In this sense, while more welfare families are leaving the rolls and working, they are not leaving poverty, in part because of low wages and unstable employment opportunities.

Moreover, this economic shift from boom to bust occurred at the same time that many families were facing their lifetime limit for receiving public aid. Welfare reform has certainly impacted the rise of family homelessness in recent years, especially for single-mother households. Temporary Assistance to Needy Families (TANF) benefits are way below the federal poverty line and insufficient for families to meet the cost of living.[26] Furthermore, only about 40% of families eligible for cash assistance from TANF actually receive it.[27] Also, with most housing subsidies unavailable for families leaving the welfare rolls, housing costs become unsustainable, causing many families to end up homeless and back on the welfare rolls.

As the current economic horizon grows dimmer, millions more Americans stand to be pushed into poverty. Already, indicators of poverty show a deepening crisis: over 36 million people now participate in the Supplemental Nutrition Assistance Program (SNAP), formerly known as the Food Stamp Program, increasing 24% in the last year alone.[28] Between September 2006 and October 2009, the unemployment rate for workers over age 25 who lack a high school diploma— already a very low-income group—increased from 6.3% to 15.5%, while the national unemployment rate reached 10.2% in October 2009. Given that unemployment rate, it is estimated that the ranks of the poor could swell by up to 10 million and the very poor by 6 million.[29] In New York City, the unemployment rate rose to 10.3% in October 2009, up from 4.8% in December 2007.[30] As poverty grows, the number of families and children forced from their homes will undoubtedly grow, too, increasing the pressure for government to find effective solutions to homelessness.

What Can Be Done

Insufficient education, domestic violence, foster care, teen pregnancy, unemployment, and welfare reform together place an overwhelming burden on a homeless family and the family shelter system in particular. As we have seen, these problems do not exist in isolation, but intersect in the web of family poverty. More and more, to be poor in this country frequently means that it is only a matter of time before homelessness begins. And as poverty continues to increase, in all likelihood, so too will family homelessness. The American economy officially entered a recession in December of 2007, and already its effects on family homelessness can be measured: in fiscal year 2009, the number of families seeking shelter in New York City increased by 21%, compared to fiscal year 2008.[31]

As daunting as these problems are for these families, the scars may be more long-lasting for their children. Homelessness intrudes upon every aspect of childhood, including education, health, and emotional well-being. Already we are seeing a second generation of the homeless: children who came of age in foster care or the shelter system of the 1980s and now are seeking shelter with children of their own. The best way to end this cycle is to focus on the needs of today's homeless children and recognize that homelessness has become their issue.

Notes

[1] Institute for Children and Poverty, Institute for Children and Poverty Data.

[2] Ibid.

[3] Ibid.

[4] Ibid.

[5] Ibid.

[6] New York State Department of Family Assistance, *Domestic Violence: Frequently Asked Questions on Reimbursement, General and Programmatic Issues* (New York: New York State Department of Family Assistance, 30 September 2002).

[7] Institute for Children and Poverty, Institute for Children and Poverty Data.

[8] Institute for Children and Poverty, *Déjà vu* (New York: Institute for Children and Poverty, 2001).

[9] M.A. Straus, R. J. Gelles, and C. Smith, *Physical Violence in American Families: Risk Factors and Adaptations to Violence in 8,145 Families* (New Brunswick: Transaction Publishers, 1990).

[10] *Mayor's Management Reports*, 2001–2009, Human Resources Administration.

[11] Mayor's Office to Combat Domestic Violence, Domestic Violence Third Quarter Fact Sheet, 2009.

[12] Institute for Children and Poverty, Institute for Children and Poverty Data.

[13] Ibid.

[14] Center for an Urban Future, "Watching the Numbers," *Child Welfare Watch (17)*, 2009.

[15] Institute for Children and Poverty National Family Homeless Database.

[16] Ibid.

[17] Institute for Children and Poverty, *Children Having Children* (New York: Institute for Children and Poverty, 2001).

[18] Ibid.

[19] Ibid.

[20] Ibid.; Institute for Children and Poverty, Data.

[21] Ibid.

[22] U.S. Census Bureau, Annual Social and Economic (ASEC) Supplement, *Years of School Completed by Poverty Status—All Races, Below 185% of Poverty.* (Washington, DC: Current Population Survery, 2006); Institute for Children and Poverty, Institute for Children and Poverty Data. Data includes high school graduates and GED recipients.

[23] New York City Human Resources Administration, *HRA Facts*, http://www.nyc.gov/html/hra/html/downloads/pdf/hrafacts_2009_08.pdf.

[24] The Center on Budget and Policy Priorities reports that those who find jobs after welfare typically earn between $8,000–$10,000 annually, well below the $14,129 poverty line for a family of three.

[25] Kay S. Hymowitz, "How Welfare Reform Worked," *City Journal*, Spring 2006.

[26] The National Coalition for the Homeless estimates that the median TANF benefit for a family of three is approximately one third of the poverty level.

[27] Sharon Parrott, "Recession Could Cause Large Increases in Poverty and Push Millions Into Deep Poverty" (Washington, D.C.: Center on Budget and Policy Priorities, 24 November 2008).

[28] Department of Agriculture, Food and Nutrition Service, "Supplemental Nutrition Assistance Program: Program Data," http://www.fns.usda.gov/pd/34SNAPmonthly.htm.

[29] Parrott, "Recession Could Cause Large Increases in Poverty and Push Millions Into Deep Poverty."

[30] New York State Department of Labor, "Local Area Unemployment Statistics Program: New York City," no longer available online.

[31] New York City Department of Homeless Services, *Critical Activities Report, Fiscal Years, 2008–2009.*

8 | **A POVERTY OF YOUTH**
Homeless Children Today

For most children, homelessness is not a brief or singular experience, but a period fraught with educational and emotional setbacks that can last for years. There are over 16,000 children currently in New York City's shelter system, and they constitute almost 43% of the entire homeless population.[1] These children endure turbulent living situations, family violence, health problems, and instability in nearly every aspect of their lives.

Education

It is no surprise that homeless children struggle in school. In New York City, 51% of all homeless children are of school age. Nearly a quarter of

Figure 29
Educational Setbacks among Homeless Children, New York City
Source: Institute for Children and Poverty Data; n=266

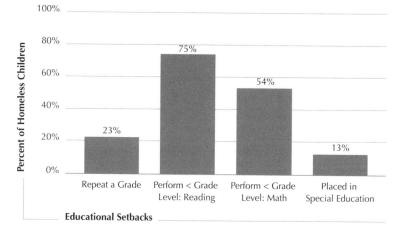

these children repeat a grade, three-quarters perform below grade level in reading, and over half perform below grade level in math.[2] Moreover, 13% have been placed in special education classes, a rate one-third higher than the average for school-aged children nationally (see Figure 29).[3]

Enrollment, Transfers, and Absences

Homeless children move sixteen times more often than the average American family, resulting in frequent school transfers, enrollment problems, and excessive absences.[4] Despite revisions to the federal McKinney-Vento Homeless Assistance Act to address these issues, the problem remains.[5] Although the new legislation allows students to remain in their home districts, transferring schools when entering shelter is all too common. In New York City, 42% of students transferred schools at least once within a single year, and of these, 21% transferred twice or more (see Figure 30).[6]

Figure 30
Homeless Children School Transfers in a Single Year, New York City
Source: Institute for Children and Poverty, Institute for Children and Poverty Data; *n=166*

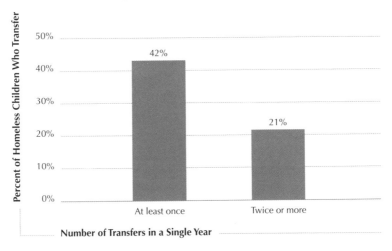

The effects of such transfers can be long-lasting. Researchers estimate that it takes a child four to six months to recover academically from such moves.[7] In fact, homeless children who transfer schools are

31% more likely to have poor attendance records than those who did not transfer at all.[8] This can also stand in the way of special education placements—multiple moves leave little time for assessment, creating a double-edged sword for homeless children with special needs, who are less likely to receive those services.

The McKinney-Vento amendment undoubtedly made positive strides for homeless children, not only by allowing them to stay in their school of origin, but also by requiring schools to enroll children even if they lack immunizations, prior school records, a permanent address, or an accompanying adult. But there is a flip side to the legislation that is negatively affecting homeless children in urban areas. If children do not transfer, they often face arduous travel to and from their home district. One study found that 34% of school-aged children in New York City spend one hour or more traveling to and from school, some journeying from southern Queens, near Kennedy airport, all the way to the upper Bronx or Harlem (see Figure 31).[9] Such long trips are not only taxing for children—some as young as first grade—but they are also spending valuable time on trains or buses when they could be attending after-school programs and getting help with their homework.

Figure 31
School Travel Times for Homeless Children (New York City, 2002)
Source: Institute for Children and Poverty Data; *n=144*

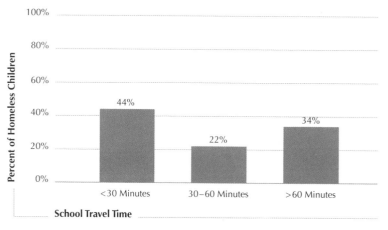

Ensuring that homeless children are actually attending school is another challenge. Regular school attendance is imperative for academic success, yet with frequent moves and frequent illnesses, 45% nationwide do not attend school regularly.[10] In New York City, 37% of homeless children miss at least two weeks of school per year, and 33% miss more than one month.[11] The impact of this can be devastating—two-thirds of students who miss twenty or more school days in one year during first, second, or third grade eventually drop out.[12] That, coupled with the fact that in New York City, more than half of all homeless children who are in grades one through three experience chronic absenteeism, makes the likelihood of eventually dropping out of school a real possibility for thousands of homeless children.

The Youngest Learners

For the younger siblings of these school-age children, education is equally critical to their future success. Yet despite recent research demonstrating the importance of cognitive development during these formative years, the U.S. Department of Education estimates that only 21% of homeless children are enrolled in preschool programs, less than half the rate of all children nationally.[13] Without preschool, these children are missing a window of opportunity for early learning and the chance to offset developmental delays. As a result, the youngest of the homeless are three times as likely to manifest such delays as non-homeless children (see Figure 32).[14] In fact, three-quarters of homeless children under age five have at least one major developmental delay, mostly speech problems.[15] Emotional and behavioral problems are also more predominant in young homeless children, with one in five warranting professional intervention, and 12% suffering from clinically diagnosed anxiety, depression, or withdrawal.[16]

Unprepared Parents

Parents play a pivotal role in promoting their children's education, but given homeless parents' own obstacles in life and educational hurdles, they often feel too unprepared and intimidated to become involved in their child's schooling. Forty-five percent have no high school or GED

Figure 32

Preschool Enrollment and Developmental Delays of Homeless vs. Non-homeless Children

Source: Rafferty & Rollins; U.S. Department of Education; Federal Interagency Forum on Child and Family Statistics

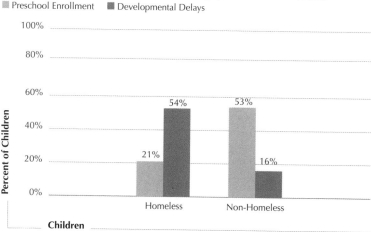

■ Preschool Enrollment   ■ Developmental Delays

diploma, and the typical homeless parent reads at a sixth grade level.[17] The majority of homeless parents do not or cannot read daily to their children, nor are they able to provide effective assistance on school assignments. Without the guidance of their parents, children are more likely to fall behind: homeless children whose parents did not graduate from high school are 47% more likely to repeat a grade and 36% are more likely to be in special education classes than those whose parents did graduate.[18]

Children's Health

Irregular sleep schedules, inadequate living situations, constant relocations, and poor nutrition all take their toll on the physical and emotional health of a homeless child. These children get sick at a rate that far outpaces other children of all income levels. Forty-six percent of the city's homeless children experience a decline in health after becoming homeless. They suffer three times as many gastrointestinal disorders, get diarrhea five times as often, 50% more ear infections, and twice as many hospitalizations as their non-homeless counterparts.[19]

Asthma appears to be one of the most enduring results of homelessness and the primary health problem these children face. Across the country, one fifth of all homeless children have asthma, almost three times the national average. In New York City, it is even more prevalent, affecting 38% of homeless children, more than four times the national rate.[20] These rates represent the highest prevalence of asthma ever reported in any child population.[21]

Since most homeless children lack a primary care physician, small, treatable, problems can easily spiral out of control. Ailments like ear infections, common to all small children, are more prevalent among homeless children, and often go untreated, eventually resulting in permanent hearing impairment. Additionally, one report noted that more than 60% of two- and three-year-old children in the New York shelter system had not been immunized against measles, mumps, and whooping cough, all preventable diseases.[22] Letting treatable illnesses go untreated is not only directly harmful to a child's health, but also impacts their school attendance, setting these children up for academic failure.

Homeless and Hungry

In addition to other health problems, homelessness increases a child's chance of experiencing hunger. A poor or insufficient diet can be extremely harmful to children's emotional and physical well-being, as well as their future health, development, and academic achievement.[23] Nationwide, one out of every five homeless children does not eat enough, and almost half of those who eat less after becoming homeless show a decline in physical health. In New York City, 19% go hungry, a rate more than four times that of non-homeless children (see Figure 33).[24] Ultimately, a lack of adequate nutrition increases the likelihood of educational and emotional setbacks, impacting their ability to develop into healthy, independent adults.

Emotional Well-being

Nearly half of all school-age children, and one in four under the age of five, experience symptoms of depression, anxiety, or aggression after becom-

Figure 33
Hunger: Homeless vs. Non-homeless Children
Source: U.S. Department of Agriculture; Institute for Children and Poverty Data; *n=3797*

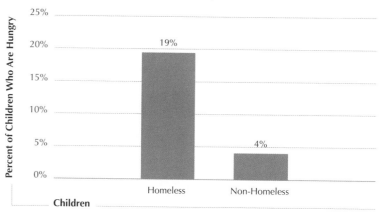

ing homeless. In New York City these emotional problems are even more pronounced, with 41% suffering emotionally after homelessness, and 19% being taunted in school (see Figure 34).[25] Considering the chaotic nature of

Figure 34
Emotional Well-Being of Homeless Children, New York City vs. National
Source: Institute for Children and Poverty Data

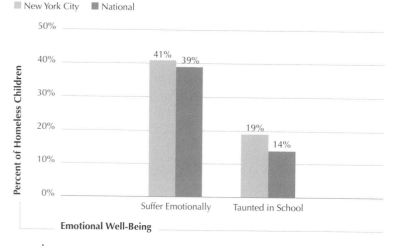

homelessness, it is no wonder that these children have emotional difficulties. Moreover, they have to contend with being teased at school; homeless children often ride the "homeless bus" and are taunted when they get to school, told that their clothes smell like a shelter or that they have no home. Such negative emotions are dangerous; researchers report that suicidal tendencies are common among homeless children over the age of five.[26]

Putting It Together: Health and School Performance

Whether children are sick, hungry, or depressed has a direct impact on their ability to concentrate and do well in school. Constant upheaval leads to more frequent illnesses and more school absences. Research shows that inadequate diets can jeopardize brain growth and cognitive development.[27]

Moreover, these problems can trigger another—hungry children are more likely to act out their aggression in the classroom, while asthmatic children are more likely to miss school, leading both groups to perform poorly academically. And the more often a child is homeless, the greater the risk for emotional and physical problems, as well as missed educational opportunities.

As devastating as these findings may be, many of the setbacks caused by homelessness may not be apparent for years to come. Children who fail to thrive at age three may be left back at age eight, and drop out of school completely by age sixteen. Every child requires stability and support to succeed in life, and homeless children are far less likely to receive either.

What Can Be Done and Where Can We Do It?

New York City must explore how to best ensure that shelters are meeting the needs of children and their families. While there is perhaps no single cure-all for homelessness, steps can be taken so that the city's homeless system is better able to prevent and respond to poverty and the lack of housing. Only then can we ensure that the homeless children of today do not inherit a legacy of severe poverty and chronic homelessness tomorrow.

We have already seen how today's families entering the shelter system struggle more with domestic violence, lack of education, and unemployment than their counterparts of over two decades ago. We have also seen how their housing options have dwindled away, as the government has retreated from its commitment to low-income affordable housing. As the situation for families has changed, many shelters have also evolved, recognizing that programs and services must reflect the current reality.

Families are now staying longer in shelters, some for periods of up to two years or more. During this time, mothers can build their parenting skills or obtain their GED, and children can get after-school tutoring and primary health services.

For the time being at least, shelters must be viewed as a new beginning rather than a last resort, and they must be made more responsive and pragmatic. The final chapter details a new vision for utilizing the powers of a shelter and transforming shelter institutions into true communities of opportunity. Such a vision and transition is the only way New York City and the nation can begin to reduce family homelessness once and for all.

Notes

[1] New York City Department of Homeless Services, Daily Report, Nov. 23, 2009.

[2] Institute for Children and Poverty, *Miles to Go: The Flip Side of the McKinney-Vento Homeless Assistance Act* (New York: Institute for Children and Poverty, January 2003).

[3] Institute for Children and Poverty, *Homeless in America: A Children's Story* (New York: Institute for Children and Poverty, 1999), 13.

[4] Sheridan Bartlet, "The Significance of Relocation for Chronically Poor Families in the USA," *Environment and Urbanization 9*, no. 1 (1997): 122.

[5] In 2001, Congress reauthorized the Stewart B. McKinney Homeless Assistance Act and renamed it the McKinney-Vento Act, in honor of the efforts of the late Representative Bruce Vento from Minnesota.

[6] Institute for Children and Poverty, *Miles to Go*.

[7] Laurene M. Heyback and Patricia Nix-Hodes, "Reducing Mobility: Good for Kids, Good for Schools," *The Beam: The Newsletter of the National Association for the Education of Homeless Children and Youth 9*, no. 1 (1999): 5.

[8] Institute for Children and Poverty, *Homeless in America*, 13.

[9] Institute for Children and Poverty, *Miles to Go*.

[10] Institute for Children and Poverty, *Homeless in America*, 13.

[11] Institute for Children and Poverty, *Miles to Go*.

[12] Heyback and Nix-Hodes, "Reducing Mobility: Good for Kids, Good for Schools," 5.

[13] Institute for Children and Poverty, *Homeless in America*, 11.

[14] Yvonne Rafferty and Norma Rollins, *Learning in Limbo: The Educational Deprivation of Young Homeless Children* (New York: Advocates for Children of New York, Inc. 1989), 39.

[15] Roy Grant, "The Special Needs of Homeless Children: Early Intervention at a Welfare Hotel," *Topics in Early Childhood Special Education* 10, no. 49 (1990): 76–91.

[16] Ellen Hart-Shegos, *Homelessness and Its Effects on Children.* Prepared for the Family Housing Fund, December 1999, 5.

[17] Institute for Children and Poverty, Institute for Children and Poverty Data.

[18] Institute for Children and Poverty, *Homeless in America,* 14.

[19] Megan Sandel, Joshua Sharfstein, and Randy Shaw, *There's No Place Like Home: How America's Housing Crisis Threatens Our Children* (San Francisco: Housing America, 1999), 8–9.

[20] Bob Herbert, "In America; Children in Crisis," *New York Times,* 10 June 1999; See also: "Still in Crisis: The Health Status of New York's Homeless Children," a publication of the Children's Health Fund.

[21] Herbert, "In America; Children in Crisis."

[22] Ibid.

[23] America's Second Harvest, *Who We Serve/Hunger: The Faces & Facts, Health and Social Consequences* (Chicago: America's Second Harvest, 1999).

[24] Institute for Children and Poverty, *Homeless in America,* 19.

[25] Ibid., 17.

[26] Mark Rosenman and Mary Lee Stein, "Homeless Children: A New Vulnerability," *Homeless Children: The Watchers and Waiters* (Binghamton: Haworth Press, 1990), 95.

[27] Irwin Redlener, *Still In Crisis: The Health Status of New York's Homeless Children* (New York: Children's Defense Fund, 1999).

9 | New Communities of Opportunity
A Vision

Almost 700,000 families, with more than one and a half million children, will be homeless in America this year. That's 1 in every 50 American children, and the numbers are growing.[1] We have seen how officials in one city responded to this crisis, trying one makeshift solution after another, from Emergency Assistance Units to congregate shelters, from welfare hotels to cluster-site housing. Yet these measures only address one aspect of homelessness — a lack of housing — and not its root causes. As a result, the number of homeless families continues to grow, shelters remain at capacity, and new facilities open regularly.

Twenty-five years ago, city shelters were no place for any family to call home. Their basic mission was simply emergency housing and little more. As a result, families remained entrenched in poverty, and many became homeless for a second, third, or even fourth time. New York City's shelter recidivism rate was a full 50%, and many of today's shelter residents themselves came of age within the emergency shelters that defined the period.[2]

More than two decades later, shelters are still here, but many have evolved into very different places — dynamic, multi-service centers addressing the comprehensive needs of homeless families. With very little affordable housing being built, shelters have become one of the only housing options that low-income families have. In fact, they may be the twenty-first century's version of low-income housing.

As we attempt to end the cycle of family homelessness, the answer may lie in these facilities of the new millennium, shelters turned into "communities of opportunity." Shelters and transitional housing have become powerful places where enormous changes in people's lives and habits can and are taking place. They either are, or can be, residential educational training centers where families live and participate in programs addressing the root causes of poverty. In fact, today these facilities are at the forefront of the war on poverty, fighting domestic violence, teen pregnancy, illiteracy, illness, and foster care placements, while simultaneously providing job readiness, employment training, and education, all on-site.

Indeed, shelters have become the new "main streets" of poor communities, serving as an alternative approach to providing community services in a residential setting under one roof. And why not? If shelters have become more permanent than ever before, and in many ways are taking the place of old, newly gentrified neighborhoods, then their power should be harnessed and their potential to transform people's lives recognized.

Some argue that this view of a shelter is misguided, acting as a barrier to the construction of permanent housing, but we must ask the fundamental question: when will this housing be built? Whether intentionally or not, government has essentially abandoned its commitment to low-income housing. Today, when government speaks of affordable housing, the question remains — affordable for whom? New York City's initiative to develop three hundred units of affordable housing in downtown Manhattan is a perfect example: qualifying applicants must earn between $50,000 and $85,000 annually. No low-income families meet that criterion, and homeless families never will. For the time being, shelters are all that is left. They have become surrogate low-income housing where poor families presently reside and will probably continue to do so for the foreseeable future. And if, as we have seen, homelessness is more complex than just housing, shelter communities can play a highly significant role in reducing family homelessness itself.

Shelters and Learning

A lack of education lies at the heart of today's poverty problems. One half of homeless parents have not completed high school, limiting not only their own potential, but also rendering them less able to promote their children's educational development.

An investment in homeless parents is also an investment in homeless children, and shelter communities are places where parents have a chance to connect with their children in ways they may never have before. Parenting classes, parent-child activities, and on-site childcare are among the programs giving parents insight into their children's emotional, physical, and intellectual development, and helping them become more active and engaged mothers and fathers. Parent-child literacy programs, like the "Together In Learning" model piloted in several New York shelters and shelters in fifteen other cities nationwide, enable parents to further their own literacy level while engaging in games, stories, and literacy projects with their children.[3] For the first time, young homeless parents are gaining the skills to become their children's first teachers, and later, to become advocates in their classrooms. With nearly half of the nation lacking the basic reading skills necessary to function in our society, shelters can become important frontline vehicles for supporting literacy efforts.[4]

At the same time as parents are making these crucial educational strides, we can ensure that their children do the same. If we are to prevent yet another generation of children from becoming homeless parents themselves, we must recognize the issues they face and address them early and comprehensively. As we have seen, homeless children have profound educational, health, and emotional needs that must be met through early intervention and ongoing educational support. With shelter stays getting longer for families, homeless children have come to know a shelter as their "home," and it is in this "home" that they receive support, encouragement, and guidance as they embark on their educational journey.

In New York City, over half of all homeless children change schools at least once a year, resulting in months of academic setbacks. They miss weeks of classes because of homelessness and are held back and wrongly placed in remedial programs. Moreover, many of them spend over an hour traveling to and from school, and many are regularly taunted for being homeless by their classmates. These are hardly the ingredients for academic success.

There is proof that focusing on the needs of these children results in remarkable academic, social, and emotional gains. A study of a New York City shelter-based after-school program found that children made significant academic gains in as little as six months, with 59% improving their overall grade-point average and 60% and 56% showing increases in their reading and math scores, respectively (see Figure 35).[5] Not only do their grades improve, so does their self-confidence and behavior: over three quarters of these children feel better about their own abilities since attending the program and 83% are more cooperative.[6]

Figure 35
Homeless Children Enrolled in After-school Programs: Grade Improvement by Academic Subject
Source: Institute for Children and Poverty; *n=95*

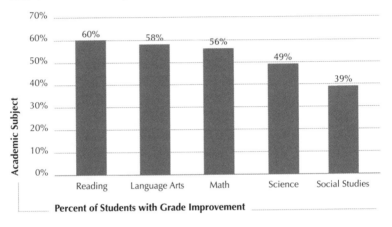

Furthermore, shelter-based educational enrichment activities have a positive impact on school attendance and parental involvement. One study found that 92% of homeless children in after-school programs have a high rate of daily school attendance, compared to only 63% of those not attending such programs. In addition, these programs have proved beneficial in helping homeless parents form partnerships with their children's schools — parents with children enrolled in these programs are more likely to visit their children's school and participate in parent-teacher forums, than parents whose children are not attending these programs.[7]

For younger children, preschool programs in shelter communities have had an enormous impact on their social, emotional, and developmental growth. In as little as eight weeks, homeless children attending preschool have demonstrated dramatically improved language skills, longer attention spans, more cooperative behavior, and greater self-confidence.[8] While it is widely acknowledged that preschool programs are an important precursor for academic success, for many of these children, this is the first time they have had access to them, as many of these programs are more readily available in a shelter community than in their old neighborhoods.

Shelters and Employment

With few homeless parents having employment experience and fewer having graduated from high school, we must initiate educational programs within shelters and teach the writing and math skills necessary for success in the workplace.[9]

Shelters should include education and GED preparation, mentoring and skill building, and job internships and actual employment, both on-site and in the community. For underemployed parents, who usually have held only brief, part-time positions, the emphasis is on gaining the skills to embark on a more viable career path. For those with work experience, the emphasis is on job retention and advancement. Shelters can become the equivalent of an educational campus, where some parents "major" in computers, while others prepare to become home daycare providers; where some are trained as security officers, and others become teacher's aides or maintenance workers. The possibilities are endless.

If the goal is to move people from public assistance to work and to end homelessness, then we have the opportunity to provide the tools to make it happen. And in a shelter-turned-community we can begin this process. It is time to take seriously the opportunity to deal with the poverty problems homeless families currently face and to do so where they currently live, in the shelter communities that exist within larger communities.

Shelters and Foster Care

With almost one third of today's shelter residents having spent some part of their childhood in foster and limbo care and many moving directly from the foster care system into the shelter system, there is an immediate need to prevent their children from following the same path.[10]

One approach is Family Respite Centers, which provide twenty-four-hour, seven-day-a-week temporary placements for children at risk of abuse or neglect. Parents deal with emergencies and sort out stressful situations that put their child at risk, and a whole new way of handling crises is learned. Through after-care and support services, respite center staff works with each family to ensure their long-term stability, keeping families together in a safe and nurturing environment. In the end, it is not just the children and their families who benefit, but the public as well: a foster care placement can cost up to $107,540 per child annually, while the annual cost of the shelters' crisis service is approximately $1,200 per child.[11] Family respite centers can offer powerful alternatives, and within the larger network of services available in the shelter-turned-community, they can prevent a lifetime of dependency within the foster care system.

Shelters and Teen Pregnancy

Many homeless heads of household had their first child while still a teenager and more than half are themselves the products of adolescent childbearing.[12] Most of these young mothers may lack the maturity and the skills to make good parenting decisions and manage their lives. For this group, most of whom dropped out of high school, educational programs can help establish goals and direction, while allowing them to gain a sense of their own potential—natural incentives to family planning and the postponement of future childbearing. They can attend GED classes to complete their schooling as well as participating in job readiness, employment training, and parenting skills workshops. They can learn that education and work are important precursors to having children, successfully raising a family, and ensuring that their children have a solid foundation for the future. And they can begin to do this all within the residential educational environment of a shelter-turned-community.

Shelters and Domestic Violence

Almost half of all homeless parents have a history of domestic violence, and nearly a third of homeless children have witnessed it. Boys who witness domestic violence are two times as likely to become abusers themselves.[13] In fact, many homeless families cite domestic violence as their primary reason for becoming homeless.

With these victims entering the shelter system at increasing rates, there is an immediate opportunity to tackle this problem in a safe and nurturing environment. A mother can access supportive services to address both her physical and emotional health within the stable, safe shelter environment. Her children can have the opportunity to address the emotional ramifications of living in an abusive household; educational and social programs provide the support they need to fully recover.

Shelters and Children's Health

Homeless children are sick more frequently and have significantly higher rates of hunger than their non-homeless counterparts. In New York City, almost three-quarters of all homeless families have no primary care physician, instead utilizing emergency rooms and walk-in clinics for their medical care.[14]

Shelters should, and many do, have on-site medical services, nutrition classes, and exercise programs. They connect parents and children to services in hospitals. For those services not available on-site, shelters could partner with local health providers and other community organizations. For the first time, these families have access to the primary care services that are critical for staying healthy, as well as resources that promote a healthy lifestyle.

Shelters and Community

Part of the power of a shelter-turned-community is the potential for positive collaborations with the larger community. Local libraries, community colleges, museums, and cultural institutions can help enhance a shelter's services and provide extracurricular activities. Children can be connected to mentors at a high school, receive one-on-one academic assistance at a library, and find a place in the spotlight in a local theater troupe. Adults can be linked to employment opportunities with community businesses and take their first steps on the road to independent living. In fact, New York City is rich with access to such opportunities; and with a shelter recognized as a new community within the larger community, all kinds of needs can be met.

Shelters are much more than just temporary housing. Many have become visionary residential community centers handling front-line poverty and dealing it a powerful blow. These new communities, partnering with the broader community, offer enormous benefits to those in need, and they do so at a reasonable cost. In New York City, the estimated cost of a shelter-turned-community is roughly $35 per person per day, including housing, education, childcare, and a full spectrum of programs and activities.[15]

In addition to cost, these communities offer families a safer, more respectable living environment than the congregate emergency shelters that preceded them. With private living suites, indoor and outdoor play areas, computer labs, and classrooms, the atmosphere is one of a community center rather than a stark city shelter. These residences are essentially "one stop shops," where all the programs and services a family needs to move forward are found under one roof.

Furthermore, this on-site approach, coupled with positive reinforcement from shelter residents and counselors, removes many of the traditional obstacles to program participation. The logistical nightmares of attempting to participate in educational and social programs, historically spread throughout the community, are gone. The search for transportation and childcare no longer stands in the way. Parents and children simply have to walk down the hall or go up the stairs to participate in services that will change their lives. Such is the power of a shelter community—veritable factories of success.

This is an approach already proven successful. In New York City, many transitional-housing Tier II facilities are working to address poverty and homelessness in new and dynamic ways. Shelters have transformed into communities of opportunity, where shelter directors advocate for resources for their residents just as elected officials do for their constituents, and staff members link families to a variety of education and employment options just as guidance counselors do for their students.

Simply put, turning shelters into communities of opportunity is an approach that works. It is truly the first step to ending family homelessness as we have known it. Families who partake in the power of a shelter are able to overcome their homelessness, move into new homes, and stay housed. Already, thousands of families who have come through these new communities have found housing and secure jobs, while furthering their education and strengthening their families. They have emerged from homelessness largely because of a commonsense approach that takes a negative circumstance and transforms it into a positive opportunity for success.

A city government, which for so long has tried to curtail and deal with the growth of family homelessness, has unexpectedly laid the groundwork to effectively reduce it permanently. This is not enough; it now needs to take the next step forward. In New York City, where the Bloomberg administration has proposed a plan with innovative initiatives to reduce poverty, the moment could not be better to effectively tackle family homelessness as well. However, it demands broader thinking. For all that has been tried to reduce family homelessness in New York City, the government still hasn't grasped the big picture. Instead of simply pushing homeless families out the door with a one- to two-year rental subsidy that does little more than delay for many the inevitable — a return to shelter when the subsidy ends — why not replace vouchers with real and meaningful work? New York City should institute a public works program on the order of the Comprehensive Employment Training Act (CETA) of 1973. CETA, a federal jobs program, helped to reduce poverty by providing unemployed, underemployed, and other economically disadvantaged individuals with job training that included classroom training, on-the-job training, work experience, and job placement assistance.

With a new public works initiative, homeless heads of household could learn a range of employment skills from clerical to trades. They would be assigned real work that develops meaningful and employable job skills and behavior, beyond menial labor, as is typically the case. These families would continue to reside in transitional housing — new communities of opportunity — with all the necessary support services to ease the transition from a lifetime of dependency on public assistance to the independence of work and self-sufficiency. At the end of their work program, a team of shelter-based employment specialists would help them move from their public works employment to a well-paying job in the private sector. Simultaneously, housing specialists would help families move from their shelter-based community of opportunity to permanent housing in new communities. Isn't it better to have families work for pay and gain employable job skills than to simply continue their dependency on temporary rental subsidies? The time is right, the infrastructure is in place, and the opportunities to end family homelessness in new and effective ways abound. As much as the New York City government may be in denial and not want to recognize it—a shelter is a home and can be an important tool to end family homelessness permanently.

In fact, the Tier II shelter system in New York City is a national model for effectively managing homelessness. The only drawback is that few people readily recognize it for what it truly is—one of the most ambitious and comprehensive anti-poverty programs ever launched by a local municipality. These facilities have harnessed all of the previously-dispersed community-based services and redeployed them in new, innovative, and cost-effective ways within temporary communities. But they are temporary in that they are only the first step. The steps in this transition are similar to those all young people take after graduating from school—they move away from home, become independent, get their first job, and rent their first apartment. At the beginning, their living arrangements and their employment may not be ideal; however, as they develop more skills, ranging from those for clerical jobs to trade jobs, they are better able to move up and out of one community into another.

In the early 1980s, the Reagan administration set all of this in motion when it began eliminating funding for low-income housing. The dissipation of this funding ensured that court-mandated integrated housing for the poor would be kept away from urban and suburban middle-class neighborhoods. If you don't have money, you can't build the housing, and if you don't have the housing, they can't come. From that day forward it was clear that it was only a matter of time before the poor were living in places other than traditional low-income housing; today's family shelter system was born. Shelters became the supposed temporary alternative, springing up in dilapidated industrial or residential areas. But twenty-five years later, they are both more permanent and more numerous than ever. Still, it would not be until the Clinton presidency and the tenure of HUD Secretary Andrew Cuomo that the federal government would play an active role in enhancing shelters and their services by supporting transitional housing and the funding of a complete continuum of care. More services were added to make shelters more humane, and the whole nature of a shelter began to change.

Today, there is a common response to homelessness — a Ten-Year Plan coming out of Washington, D.C. It purports to end homelessness by closing the so-called "front door." By closing shelters and dismantling programs, the plan expects the homeless to be absorbed into other existing service systems. It is, in fact, reminiscent of the 1980s "just say no" anti-drug and teen pregnancy campaigns, illogical approaches that do nothing about a problem except expect it to disappear. The Ten-Year Plan is already eight years old and little has changed: the homeless keep coming, and only lip service is paid to the development of new low-income housing. Truth be told, without a massive, immediate infusion of truly affordable housing for the poor, no plan, regardless of its timetable, can succeed. And with the national government functioning in both a deep recession and wartime economy, with national and local deficits estimated to be in the trillions of dollars, it is inconceivable that any such initiative can be taken. In reality, the Ten-Year Plan is already dated, and represents an abdication of responsibility rather than a viable solution to the multi-faceted problem of homelessness.

Instead, those truly concerned with ending family homelessness are at a crossroads. They could, and should, continue to advocate for new housing, understanding that it still remains a long-term goal. They could also abandon viable solutions, and buy into the Ten-Year Plan, discovering several years from now that they have helped to usher in a new generation of homeless. Or they could recognize the true breadth and depth of the problem, work within the environment and infrastructure already in place, and deal a powerful blow against family homelessness and severe poverty.

This book has chronicled the history and reality of family homelessness in New York City, but the problems and solutions are similar everywhere; only the magnitude of the problem differs. After twenty-five years, New York's homeless policies have come complete circle, and family homelessness today is far worse than when the Bloomberg administration first tackled it almost eight years ago. Yet New York City has inadvertently developed a viable framework for ending family homelessness; it is now up to government officials and the public to recognize it and put it to work. Simply put, if we are ever going to end family homelessness as we have known it, we have to realize that it will take a community to do so — a new community of opportunity — which begins in shelters themselves. If we don't build one, we will be faced with yet another generation of homeless families and children, idling in shelters across this country, waiting for the housing that may never come. For the time being at least, a shelter has indeed become a home.

Notes

[1] National Center on Family Homelessness, *America's Youngest Outcasts: State Report Card on Child Homelessness* (Newton, MA, National Center on Family Homelessness, 2009).

[2] New York City Commission on the Homeless, *The Way Home: A New Direction in Social Policy* (New York: New York City Commission on the Homeless, 1992), 75.

[3] Institute for Children and Poverty, *Together in Learning Family Literacy Curriculum* (New York: Institute for Children and Poverty, 1996.)

[4] National Institute for Literacy, "Frequently Asked Questions," http://www.nifl.gov/nifl/faqs.html#literacy%20rates.

[5] Institute for Children and Poverty, *Back to the Future: The Brownstone and FutureLink After-school Programs for Homeless Children* (New York: Institute for Children and Poverty, 2001).

[6] Ibid.

[7] Ibid.

[8] Ralph Nunez, "Access to Success: Meeting the Educational Needs of Homeless Children," *Social Work In Education,* 1994.

[9] Institute for Children and Poverty, *Job Readiness: Crossing the Threshold from Homelessness to Employment* (New York: Institute for Children and Poverty, 1994).

[10] Institute for Children and Poverty, *The Hidden Migration: Why Shelters Are Overflowing with Families* (New York: Institute for Children and Poverty, 2003).

[11] *Mayor's Management Report,* Administration for Children's Services, Fiscal Year 2009. Estimate based on per diem cost per case of $294.63.

[12] Institute for Children and Poverty, *Children Having Children.*

[13] Institute for Children and Poverty, *Déjà vu;* Straus, Gelles, and Smith, *Physical Violence in American Families,* (New York: Transaction Publishers, 1989).

[14] Institute for Children and Poverty, *Déjà vu.*

[15] Estimate based on current census of three individuals per family. Per the FY2009 *Mayor's Management Report,* the per diem cost for a family placement is $105.22.

Epilogue

As this book goes to press, New York City is once again pursuing a series of policy choices that fly in the face of a rational, accountable approach to serving the best interests of homeless families and effectively reducing family homelessness. In the summer of 2009, the clock expired on the timeframe of the mayor's five-year plan *(Uniting for Solutions Beyond Shelter)* to reduce homelessness by two-thirds, sealing the city's failure to come close to the ambitious yet arbitrary goals set forth in that document. No longer constrained by the unattainable guidelines of the plan, city policy makers could have changed course and recognized family homelessness as a problem intractably woven into the fabric of the city. The New York City Department of Homeless Services (DHS) could have readjusted its priorities to focus resources on mitigating the tragedy of homelessness for each family that experiences it, while also making long-term plans for preventive structural change. Instead, DHS has already shown conclusive signs that it will continue its stubborn refusal to abandon the punitive logic that it pursued so unsuccessfully in the era of the five-year plan, and double-down on its efforts to fundamentally destabilize the ability of the city's transitional non-profit shelters to effectively deal with the root causes of homelessness and offer meaningful services to families.

This process began in early 2009, when DHS quietly announced a new set of policies designed to put further pressure on the homeless families residing in transitional shelters. These regulations included a plan to enforce a citywide "code of conduct" for shelter residents that oblige service providers to evict the most troubled families. The proposed rules would require that shelters lock families with children out of the shelter during the daytime and enforce strict curfew and behavior rules that would best be left up to the shelter providers themselves. At the same time, DHS plans to force some homeless families to pay up to 50 percent of earned income for their shelter stay and to financially penalize shelter providers if a client family is unable to find a permanent housing placement within the arbitrarily allotted time of one hundred-eighty days. Each of these policies focuses on addressing the homeless problem by penalizing and demanding immediate changes from both homeless families and service providers. This heightened accountability on those who are most vulnerable and those who provide shelter serves only to divert the public's attention from the accountability that should be most relevant: that of the city government for its erratic policies and failures to improve homeless services.

Furthermore, the idea of having shelter operators collect rent from homeless families who are trying to put together enough savings to exit the shelter system is more than illogical; it is damaging. The process puts the client in an adversarial relationship with the very persons who are trying to help them—the providers of shelter and services. The policy also raises disturbing questions about the roles and responsibilities of shelters as collectors of rent. When a homeless mother (or father) pays for his/her shelter stay, does that parent become a legal tenant with rights, residing in low-income housing with a shelter provider as the landlord? In its efforts to punish homeless families for residing in shelters, the Bloomberg administration has started the city down a legally troubling slippery slope it is sure to regret.

The city's continued reliance on punitive methods begs the question, why has the problem of homelessness proven to be so intractable in the face of so many efforts to end it? Family homelessness exists because of a complex set of social issues driven by severe poverty and compounded by a shortage of affordable housing. Surely there are families for whom homelessness is only the result of a temporary setback, but for the overwhelming majority of homeless families, their status is the product of the dismantling of the social safety net that has occurred over the last thirty years. Indeed, as poverty deepens in the current recession, homelessness is exploding across America. From Honolulu to Miami, demand for homeless shelters far exceeds capacity, and families are sleeping in abandoned buildings, and motels, or in cars and tents. The living conditions that an unknown number of children and their families experience are truly a national disgrace.

It is important to note that in New York City we have not seen these catastrophes enacted on our city streets. Because of the city's family shelter system, homeless mothers always have a place to go and never have to resort to such desperate tactics of survival. Two decades ago, the city began to invest in building non-profit transitional shelters exactly because they offered the unique ability to facilitate successful transitions for homeless families into stable housing. After years of wise municipal investment, these quality non-profit shelters continue to help families successfully rebuild their lives, and it is the "continuum of care" that they offer that has kept poverty in check.[1] They serve as a safety net that effectively manages homelessness and prevents the problem from turning into the crisis that we see in so many other parts of the country today.

Despite these accomplishments, the cumulative effect of the city's current policies is to attack the shelter system's ability to substantively aid homeless families. The proposed policy changes threaten to reduce the majority of New York's shelter system to what it was in the early '80s: a bare-bones, unaccountable collection of hotel and apartment owners without any interest in permanently reducing family homelessness other than simply to increase their profit margins. Instead of becoming members of a community of opportunity with access to health services, job training, childcare, and connections with educators and employers in the neighborhood, families will now reside in a closed, isolated system until they are ultimately rejected from it for staying too long.

At the same time, the city is undercutting its transitional, non-profit shelter system even further by diverting more and more families into non-contracted, privately-owned welfare hotels and cluster-site apartments. New York was successful in nearly eliminating the use of such facilities to shelter homeless families in the late 1990s. But today more than 2,300 families reside in welfare hotels nightly, while more than 1,500 live in what the city calls cluster-site units — a term for low-quality, service-deficient apartments rented to the city by private landlords. It could be that DHS prefers to work with the profit-making operators of these facilities because, unlike non-profit shelters, they are not regulated by state guidelines that guarantee levels of service and quality of housing. They are in fact an effective means of hiding the homeless by dispersing families throughout the city with no means of evaluating the success or failure of preparing and moving them to permanent housing. In fact, a recent *New York Times* article noted that the increased utilization of cluster-site housing is serving as a perverse incentive for landlords to reduce the amount of available low-income housing. As in the 1980s, when landlords converted single-room-occupancy buildings (SROs) into welfare hotels, today some landlords can make up to seven times more in monthly rent by pushing out their rent-stabilized tenants and converting their apartments into "cluster-site units" for newly homeless families. As a result whole buildings are being converted and former low-income tenants are now facing homelessness as a result.[2]

This book has demonstrated that the answer to reducing family homelessness is not in setting arbitrary targets to lower the shelter census. Neither is it about distracting public attention from the problem by unveiling new punitive policies while hiding homeless families in shady apartments scattered across the city. The answer can only lie with a strategy that focuses on gaining the greatest success in permanently moving homeless families from shelter into stable, long-term affordable housing. That means appropriately and effectively addressing the social problems that brought them to shelter in the first place.

If New York City proceeds with its u-turn on homeless policy, it will inadvertently, or advertently, destroy a system that effectively manages family homelessness and truly works. In the end, this will certainly return us to those less than lustrous days of yesteryear, when shame, squalor, and waste characterized the family shelter system of the later 1980s and early 90s. But it doesn't have to be that way, it shouldn't be that way; and it won't be that way if those currently overseeing the shelter system pay attention to the lessons of the past and present. A shelter may or may not be a home — that depends on one's point of view — but it is clearly an effective tool to be used to reduce family homelessness. This book has presented a blueprint for change, a blueprint based on the historical evolution of New York City's family shelters, and lessons learned and forgotten over the decades. As is said, if it isn't broken, don't try to fix it. To dismantle a functioning system for assisting vulnerable families and children with no proven replacement risks dire consequences. Instead, use those resources, build upon them, and reduce family homelessness in New York City in an effective and positive way.

Notes

[1] In the early 1990s, the Cuomo Commission advocated for a continuum of care approach, centered in shelters, to deal with the variety of issues that homeless families face. This approach recognizes that matching families with specialized services and shelters is a crucial step towards aiding recovery and avoiding waste in the system. The federal government has adopted continuum of care standards for its usage of McKinney-Vento funding: http://www.icprwb.com

[2] Julie Bosman, "Tenants Wary of Clustering of Homeless," *New York Times,* March 3, 2009.

Bibliography

Published Books, Articles, and Reports

Bartlet, Sheridan. "The Significance of Relocation for Chronically Poor Families in the USA." *Environment and Urbanization* 9, no. 1 (1997).

Basler, Barbara. "Koch Limits Using Welfare Hotels." *New York Times,* 17 December 1985.

———. "Welfare Hotels Sued Over Taxes." *New York Times,* 27 December 1985.

Bernstein, Andrea and Amy Eddings. "Handshake Hotels: Part 1." *Morning Edition,* National Public Radio. WNYC, New York, 8 October 2003.

———. "Handshake Hotels: Part 3; How a Few Big Landlords Benefit From NYC's Homeless Placement System." *Morning Edition,* National Public Radio. WNYC, New York, 8 October 2003.

Bernstein, Nina. "A Plan To End City Homelessness In 10 Years." *New York Times,* 13 June 2002.

———. "Homeless Shelters in NY Filled to the Highest Level Since '80s." *New York Times,* 8 February 2001.

———. "Many More Children Calling New York City Shelters Home." *New York Times,* 13 February 2002.

———. "Mentally Ill Boy Kills Himself in Shelter Hotel." *New York Times,* 8 August 2002.

"Bloomberg Administration Seeks More Aggressive Plan for the Homeless." Associated Press, 18 June 2002.

Bumiller, Elisabeth. "In Wake of Attack, Giuliani Cracks Down on Homeless." *New York Times,* 20 November 1999.

Burt, Martha. *Over the Edge: The Growth of Homelessness in the 1980s.* Washington, DC; Urban Institute Press, 1992.

Castro, Laura. "Bankers Trust Funds Housing for Homeless." *Newsday,* 19 August 1990.

Center on Budget and Policy Priorities. "Housing Vouchers Funded in New York Under Pending Proposals." (Washington, D.C.: Center on Budget and Policy Priorities, 1 November 2006).

Center for an Urban Future. "Watching the Numbers." *Child Welfare Watch* (15), 2008.

Coalition for the Homeless. *The Right to Shelter for Homeless New Yorkers: Twenty Years and Counting.* New York: Coalition for the Homeless, 2002.

Coates, Ta-Nehisi. "Empty Promises: Housing Activists Say the City Wastes Its Vacant Lots." *The Village Voice,* 11 March 2003.

Cooper, Michael. "Jail Reopens as a Shelter for Families." *New York Times,* 12 August 2002.

"Cuomo Makes Visit to Homeless." *New York Times,* 19 December 1985.

Daskal, Jennifer. *In Search of Shelter: The Growing Shortage of Affordable Rental Housing.* Washington, D.C.: Center on Budget and Policy Priorities, 10 June 1988.

Dolbeare, Cushing, Irene Basloe Saraf, and Sheila Crowley. *Changing Priorities: The Federal Budget and Housing Assistance 1976–2005.* Washington, D.C.: National Low Income Housing Coalition, October 2004.

Egan, Jennifer. "To Be Young and Homeless." *New York Times Magazine,* 24 March 2002.

Fernandez, Manny. "Housing Cuts Are Proposed to Close Budget Gap." *New York Times,* 30 May 2008.

Goodwin, Michael. "Carol Bellamy Fights Sharing of Apartments for Homeless Families." *New York Times,* 28 June 1984.

——. "State is Penalizing City Over Shelter Conditions." *New York Times,* 21 December 1983.

Grant, Roy. "The Special Needs of Homeless Children: Early Intervention at a Welfare Hotel." *Topics in Early Childhood Special Education* 10, no. 4 (1991): 76–91.

Grossman, Jill. "Room for Homeless Families: Can Experts Do What 20 Years of Court Couldn't?" *City Limits Magazine,* March 2002.

Haddon, Heather. "City Homeless Program Rewards Bad Landlords." *Norwood News,* 4 December 2002.

Hart-Shegos, Ellen. *Homelessness and Its Effects on Children.* Prepared for the Family Housing Fund, December 1999.

Hemphill, Clara. "The High Price of Sheltering City's Homeless." *Newsday,* 2 December 1988.

Herbert, Bob. "In America; Children in Crisis." *New York Times,* 10 June 1999.

Hewlett, Sylvia Ann. *When the Bough Breaks: The Cost of Neglecting Our Children.* New York: Basic Books, 1991.

Heyback, Laurene M. and Patricia Nix-Hodes. "Reducing Mobility: Good for Kids, Good for Schools." *The Beam* 9, no. 1 (1999).

"Homelessness Emerges as Campaign Issue for Clinton and Giuliani." CNN. 5 December 1999.

Hymowitz, Kay S. "How Welfare Reform Worked." *City Journal.* New York: City Journal, Spring 2006.

Institute for Children and Poverty. *The Challenge of Sheltering New York City's Growing Homeless Family Population: The Economic Crisis and Families in Need.* New York: Institute for Children and Poverty, forthcoming.

——. *Factsheet on Domestic Violence: Homelessness and Violence Against Women: Inside and Outside New York City.* New York: Institute for Children and Poverty, 2009.

——. *Pushed Out: The Hidden Costs of Gentrification: Displacement and Homelessness.* New York: Institute for Children and Poverty, 2009.

——. *Uncertainty at the Front Door: Homeless Families and their "Right to Shelter" in New York City.* Institute for Children and Poverty, 2009.

——. *Failure at the Four Year Mark: A Look at New York City's Plan to End Homelessness.* New York: Institute for Children and Poverty, 2008.

——. *The Instabilities of Housing Stability Plus.* New York: Institute for Children and Poverty, 2006.

——. *A Tale of Two Cities: Family Homelessness in Connecticut.* New York: Institute for Children and Poverty, 2003.

——. *Children Having Children: Teen Pregnancy and Homelessness in New York City.* New York: Institute for Children and Poverty, 2003.

——. *Miles to Go: The Flip Side of the McKinney-Vento Homeless Assistance Act.* New York: Institute for Children and Poverty, 2003.

——. *The Hidden Migration: Why New York City Shelters Are Overflowing with Families.* New York: Institute for Children and Poverty, 2002.

——. *What New Jersey Needs to Know … About Family Homelessness*. New York: Institute for Children and Poverty, 2002.

——. *A Shelter Is Not a Home … Or Is It?* New York: Institute for Children and Poverty, 2001.

——. *Back to the Future: The Brownstone and FutureLink After-school Programs for Homeless Children*. New York: Institute for Children and Poverty, 2001.

——. *Déjà vu: Family Homelessness in New York City*. New York: Institute for Children and Poverty, 2001.

——. *Multiple Families: Multiplying Problems: A First Look at the Fathers of Homeless Children*. New York: Institute for Children and Poverty, 2000.

——. *The Other America: Homeless Families in the Shadow of a New Economy — Family Homelessness in Kentucky, Tennessee and the Carolinas*. New York: Institute for Children and Poverty, 2000.

——. *A Welfare Reform-Homelessness-Foster Care Connection? The Story of "Lag Families" and "Limbo Children" in San Diego*. New York: Institute for Children and Poverty, 1999.

——. *Homeless in America: A Children's Story*. New York: Institute for Children and Poverty, 1999.

——. *Inside the Beltway: The State of Homeless Children in Washington, D.C.* New York: Institute for Children and Poverty, 1999.

——. *Day to Day … Parent to Child: The Future of Violence Among Homeless Children in America*. New York: Institute for Children and Poverty, 1998.

——. *Homeless Families Today: Our Challenge Tomorrow*. New York: Institute for Children and Poverty, 1998.

——. *Ten Cities: A Snapshot of Family Homelessness Across America, 1997–1998*. New York: Institute for Children and Poverty, 1998.

——. *The Cycle of Homelessness: A Social Policy Reader*. New York: Institute for Children and Poverty, 1998.

——. *Up the Down Staircase: A Look at Family Homelessness in New Jersey*. New York: Institute for Children and Poverty, 1998.

——. *A Trail of Tears … Trapped in a Cycle of Violence and Homelessness*. Institute for Children and Poverty, 1997.

——. *Homelessness: The Foster Care Connection*. New York: Institute for Children and Poverty, 1997.

——. *A Tale of Two Nations: The Creation of "Poverty Nomads."* New York: Institute for Children and Poverty, 1996.

——. *Common Sense: Why Jobs and Training Alone Won't End Welfare for Homeless Families in America.* New York: Institute for Children and Poverty, 1996.

——. *The Age of Confusion: Why So Many Teens are Getting Pregnant, Turning to Welfare, and Ending Up Homeless.* New York: Institute for Children and Poverty, 1996.

——. *The Dollars and Sense of Welfare: Why Work Alone Won't Work.* New York: Institute for Children and Poverty, 1996.

——. *An American Family Myth: Every Child at Risk.* New York: Institute for Children and Poverty, 1995.

——. *Job Readiness: Crossing the Threshold from Homelessness to Employment.* New York: Institute for Children and Poverty, 1994.

——. *Access to Success: Meeting the Educational Needs of Homeless Children and Families.* New York: Institute for Children and Poverty, 1993.

——. *The New Poverty: A Generation of Homeless Families.* New York: Institute for Children and Poverty, 1992.

Joint Center for Housing Studies. *The State of the Nation's Housing: 2000.* Cambridge, MA: Harvard University, 2000.

——. *The State of the Nation's Housing: 2008.* Cambridge, MA: Harvard University, 2008.

Kaufman, Leslie. "Manhattan: No Cruise Ships for Homeless." *New York Times,* 18 June 2003.

Kenning, Mary Anita Merchant, and Alan Tompkins. "Research on the Effects of Witnessing Parental Battering: Clinical and Legal Policy Implications." *Women Battering: Policy Responses.* Cincinnati, OH: Anderson, 1991.

Kozol, Jonathan. *Rachel and Her Children.* New York: Crown, 1987.

Kusmer, Kenneth. *Down and Out and On the Road: The Homeless in American History.* New York: Oxford, University Press, 2001.

Leonard, Paul, Cushing N. Dolbeare, and Edward B. Lazare. *A Place to Call Home: The Crisis in Housing for the Poor.* Washington, D.C.: Center on Budget and Policy Priorities, 1989.

Lueck, Thomas. "Breaking New Ground in Housing Policy." *New York Times,* 30 April 1989.

McMillan, Tracie. "Sleep Disorder." *City Limits,* 4 January 2001.

Mishel, Lawrence, Jared Bernstein, and John Schmitt. *The State of Working America: 1998–1999.* Washington, D.C.: Economic Policy Institute, 1999.

Mihaly, Lisa Klee. *Homeless Families: Failed Policies and Young Victims.* Washington, D.C.: The Children's Defense Fund, 1991.

National Coalition for the Homeless. *Fact Sheet #18: The McKinney Act,* April 1999.

National Jobs With Peace Campaign. *Fact Sheet.* Boston, 1990.

National Low Income Housing Coalition. *Changing Priorities: The Federal Budget and Housing Assistance 1976–2005.* Washington, D.C.: National Low Income Housing Coalition, 2004.

"New York Barred from Placing Needy Families in Midtown Hotels." Associated Press, 21 December 1986.

Nix, Crystal. "Housing Family in a Shelter Costs the City $70,000 Per Year." *New York Times,* 7 March 1986.

———. "Profits of Welfare Hotels Placing Needy Families in Midtown Hotels." Associated Press, 21 December 1986.

Nunez, Ralph. "A Shelter Is Not a Home … Or Is It? New Communities of Opportunity" in *Solutions to Homelessness,* ed. Robert McNamara, vol. 3 of *Homeless in America* (London: Praeger Perspectives, 2008), 17–29.

———. "Family Homelessness in New York City: A Case Study." *Political Science Quarterly* 116 (Fall 2001): 367–379.

———. "Breaking the Cycle: Educating America's Homeless Children." In *By Design and Neglect: The Education of Homeless and Street Children in the United States, Brazil and Cuba,* edited by J. Anyon and R.A. Mickelson. Nashville, TN: Rutledge, 2000.

———. "The Homeless in the New Era of Welfare Reform: A View from the Trenches." *Metropolitics* 1, no. 3 (Winter 1997): 14–16.

———. *The New Poverty: Homeless Families in America.* New York: Insight Books, 1996.

———. "Family Values Among Homeless Families." *Public Welfare* 53, no. 4 (Fall 1995): 24–32.

———. "Shelters Can Help the Homeless." In *The Homeless: Opposing Viewpoints,* Edited by T.L. Roleff. San Diego, CA: Greenhaven Press, Inc., 1995.

——. "Access to Success: Meeting the Educational Needs of Homeless Children." *Social Work In Education,* 1994.

——. *Hopes, Dreams, and Promise: The Future of Homeless Children in America.* New York: Homes for the Homeless, 1994.

——. "The New Poverty: A Generation of Homeless Families." *American College Journal of Business* (Spring 1992).

Nunez, Ralph and Laura M. Caruso. *The American Family Inn Handbook: A How-to Guide.* New York: White Tiger Press, 2002.

Nunez, Ralph and Kate Collignon. "Creating a Community of Learning for Homeless Children." In *Educational Leadership* 55, no. 2 (October 1997): 56–60.

Nunez, Ralph and Cybelle Fox. "A Snapshot of Family Homelessness Across America." *Political Science Quarterly* 114, no. 2 (Summer 1999): 289–307.

Nunez, Ralph and Jesse Andrews Ellison. *Moving Out, Moving Up: Families Beyond Shelter.* New York: White Tiger Press, 2006.

Nunez, Ralph and Naomi Sugie. *Beyond the Shelter Wall: Homeless Families Speak Out.* New York: White Tiger Press, 2004.

"NYC's Homeless Lockjam." Editorial. *New York Times,* 14 Aug. 2002.

O'Malley, Padraig. *Homelessness: New England and Beyond.* Amherst, MA: University of Massachusetts Press, 1992.

Olsson, Elizabeth. "A Real Estate Bargain; A Push for Expanding Supportive Housing to Stem a Growing Homeless Crisis." *City Limits,* July/August 2002.

Parrott, Sharon. "Recession Could Cause Large Increases in Poverty and Push Millions Into Deep Poverty." Washington, D.C.: Center on Budget and Policy Priorities, 24 November 2008.

Rafferty, Yvonne and Norma Rollins. *Learning in Limbo: The Educational Deprivation of Young Homeless Children.* New York: Advocates for Children of New York, Inc., 1989.

Redlener, Irwin. *Still in Crisis: The Health Status of New York's Homeless Children.* New York: The Children's Health Fund, 1999.

Reich, Robert. "As the World Turns." *The New Republic.* (28) May 1, 1989.

Renwick, Trudi. *Pulling Apart in New York: An Analysis of Income Trends in New York State.* New York: Fiscal Policy Institute, 2008.

Rice, Douglass and Barbara Sard. *Decade of Neglect Has Weakened Federal Low-Income Housing Programs*. Washington, D.C.: Center on Budget and Policy Priorities, 24 February 2009.

Rosenman, Mark and Mary Lee Stein. "Homeless Children: A New Vulnerability," *Homeless Children: The Watchers and Waiters*. Binghamton: Haworth Press, 1990.

Sandel, Megan, Joshua Sharfstein, and Randy Shaw. *There's No Place Like Home: How America's Housing Crisis Threatens Our Children*. San Francisco: Housing America, 1999.

Sard, Barbara. *Number of Homeless Climbing Due to Recession*. Washington, D.C.: Center on Budget and Policy Priorities, 8 January 2009.

Second Harvest. *Who We Serve/Hunger: The Faces & Facts, Health and Social Consequences*. Chicago: Second Harvest, 1999.

Steinhauer, Jennifer. "A Jail Becomes a Shelter, and Maybe a Mayor's Albatross." *New York Times,* 13 August 2002.

Straus, Murray Arnold, Richard J. Gelles, and Christine Smith. "Physical Violence in American Families: Risk Factors and Adaptations to Violence in 8,145 Families." New Brunswick: Transaction Publishers, 1990.

Supportive Housing Network of New York. "Funding the Solution to Homelessness: An Analysis of the New York/New York III Agreement." New York: Supportive Housing Network of New York, 2005. Available at: www.shnny.org/agreements.html.

Topousis, Tom. "Shellacked by Slumlords." *New York Post,* 19 May 2003.

———. "They Owe, We Pay." *New York Post,* 22 May 2003.

Torrey, E. Fuller. "Stop the Madness." *Wall Street Journal,* 18 July 1997.

Wilgoren, Jody. "After Welfare, Working Poor Still Struggle, Report Finds." *New York Times,* 25 April 2002.

Zucchino, David. *The Myth of the Welfare Queen*. New York: Touchstone, Simon and Schuster, 1997.

Government Documents and Reports

Independent Budget Office. *Inside the Budget.* New York: Independent Budget Office, 12 September 2002.

———. "Inside the Budget: Has the Rise in Homeless Prevention Spending Decreased the Shelter Population?" New York: Independent Budget Office, August 2008. Available at: http://www.ibo.nyc.ny.us/newsfax/insidethebudget157.pdf.

Manhattan Borough President's Task Force on Housing for Homeless Families. *A Shelter Is Not a Home.* New York: Manhattan Borough President's Task Force on Housing for Homeless Families, 1987.

Mayor's Press Office. "Mayor Giuliani Opens the Coney Island Job Center." Press Release #239–01, 5 July 2001.

New York City Commission on the Homeless. *The Way Home: A New Direction in Social Policy.* New York: New York City Commission on the Homeless, 1992.

New York City Department of Homeless Services. *Critical Activities Report, Family Services: Fiscal Year 2009.* New York: New York City Department of Homeless Services, 2009.

———. *Critical Activities Report: Fiscal Year 2008.* New York: New York City Department of Homeless Services, June 2008.

———. *Critical Activities Report, Family Services: Fiscal Year 2003.* New York: Department of Homeless Services, 2003.

———. *Critical Activities Report: Fiscal Year 2003.* New York: New York City Department of Homeless Services, January 2003.

———. *Reforming New York City's System of Homeless Services.* New York: New York City Department of Homeless Services, 1994.

———. *The Second Decade of Reform: A Strategic Plan for New York City's Homeless Services.* New York City Department of Homeless Services, 2002.

New York City Department of Housing Preservation and Development. *HPD Announces New Round of Building Blocks!* Available at: http://www.nyc.gov./html/hpd/html/pr1999/rfql-pr.shtml.

———. *2005 Housing and Vacancy Survey: Initial Findings.* New York: New York City Department of Housing Preservation and Development, 2005.

———. *2002 Housing and Vacancy Survey: Initial Findings.* New York City
    Department of Housing Preservation and Development, 2002.

———. *1999 Housing and Vacancy Survey: Initial Findings.* New York: New
    York City Department of Housing Preservation and Development, 1999.

New York City Office of the State Comptroller. *Running Out of Time: The
    Impact of Federal Welfare Reform.* New York: New York City Human
    Resources Administration, 2001.

New York City Mayor's Office of Operations. Mayor's Management Report.
    New York: City of New York, 1983, 1985-2009.

———. Preliminary Mayor's Management Report. New York: City of New York,
    2008–2009.

New York State Department of Family Assistance. *Domestic Violence:
    Frequently Asked Questions on Reimbursement, General and
    Programmatic Issues.* New York: New York State Department of Family
    Assistance, 30 September 2002.

New York State Department of Labor. "State Loses More Than 100,000
    Private Sector Jobs in Last Three Months." Available at: http://www.
    labor.state.ny.us/pressreleases/2009/Jan22_2009.htm.

Stegman, Michael. *Housing and Vacancy Report: New York City.* New York:
    Department of Housing Preservation and Development, 1987.

U.S. Census Bureau. "Poverty," 2002. Available at: http://www.census.gov/
    prod/2003pubs/p60-222.pdf.

U.S. Department of Housing and Urban Development. *Martinez, Pataki and
    Bloomberg Announce $50 million Affordable Housing Initiative in
    Lower Manhattan.* New York: U.S. Department of Housing and Urban
    Development, 2003. Available at: http://www.hud.gov/news.

———. Waiting In Vain: An Update on America's Housing Crisis. Washington,
    D.C.: U.S. Department of Housing and Urban Development 1999.

Unpublished Sources

Annie E. Casey Foundation. "KIDS COUNT." Available at: http://aecf.org.

Children's Aid Society. "History." Available at: http://www.childrensaidsociety.
    org/about/history.

Coalition for the Homeless. The Right to Shelter and Other Litigation-History.
    Available at: http://www.coalitionforthehomeless.org/righttoshelter.html.

Department of Agriculture, Food and Nutrition Service. "Supplemental Nutrition Assistance Program: Program Data." Available at http://www. fns.usda.gov/pd/34SNAPmonthly.htm.

Gibbs, Linda. "City Council Testimony." New York City Council Meeting. City Hall, New York, 18 September 2002.

New York City Human Resources Administration. *HRA Facts: January 2003.* Available at: http://www.nyc.gov/html/hra/html.hrafacts.html/. Accessed for first publication.

Institute for Children and Poverty. Unpublished Data. August 2003.

Murphy, Kenneth. Personal interview. 26 February 2002.

National Bureau of Economic Research, Bureau of Labor Statistics. New York State Department of Labor, 1992.

New York City Department of Homeless Services. "About DHS." Available at: http://www.nyc.gov/html/dhs/html/about/about_dhs.shtml. Accessed for first publication.

New York City Rent Guidelines Board. "How Can I Find Affordable Housing: Where Can You Find the Lowest Rents?" Available at: http://www. housingnyc.com/html/guide/basics_htm/#affordable. *New York Kids Need Housing!* Available at: *City Limits,* http://www.citylimits.org/content/ articles/viewarticle.cfm?article_id=2883.

Schatt, Larry. Personal interview. 8 February 2002.

Tuchelli, Sal. Personal interview. 12 April 2002.

United Neighborhood Houses. *Settlement House History.* Available at: http://www.unhny.org/about/settlement.hfn.

Wackstein, Nancy. Personal interview. 15 March 2002.

Photography Credits

Index

Page numbers in italics refer to notes (*n*), figures (*f*), illustrations (*i*), and tables (*t*).